OPEN THE BOX

BY JANE ROOT

Comedia Publishing Group
9 Poland St. London W1V 3DG
Tel: 01 439 2059

ABOUT TELEVISION
COMEDIA SERIES • Nº 34

Comedia Publishing Group was set up to investigate and monitor the media in Britain and abroad. The aim of the project is to provide basic information, investigate problem areas, and to share the experiences of those working in the field, while encouraging debate about the future development of the media. The opinions expressed in the books in the Comedia series are those of the authors, and do not necessarily relect the views of Comedia.

For a list of other Comedia titles see back pages.

First published in 1986 by Comedia Publishing Group.
© Comedia Publishing Group and Jane Root, 1986.
ISBN 0 906 890 780 (paperback)
British Library Cataloguing in Publication Data
Root, Jane
    About television.
    I. Television broadcasting—Social aspects
    I. Title
    302.2'345   HE8700.6

Cover design and book design by Andy Dark/Graphics International Tel: (01) 833 2988

Typeset by Photosetting, 6 Foundry House, Stars Lane, Yeovil, Somerset BA20 1NL. Tel. (0935) 23684.
Grassroots Typeset, 101 Kilburn Square, London NW6 6PS. Tel: (01) 328 0318.
Printed by Unwin Brothers Ltd,
The Gresham Press, Old Woking, Surrey.

Trade Distribution by George Philip Services,
Arndale Road, Wick, Littlehampton, W. Sussex BN17 7EN. Tel: 0903 717453.
Distributed in Australia by Second Back Row Press,
50 Govett St., Katoomba, N.S.W. 2780
Distributed in Canada by D.E.C. 229 College Street, Toronto, Ontario, Canada M5T 1RA.

CONTENTS

Open The Box

Produced by Beat Productions/BFI Education for Channel Four.

Directors Gina Newson, Christopher Rawlence, Mike Dibb
Series Researcher Jane Root
Film Researcher Paul Kerr
Sports Programme Researcher Gary Whannel
BFI Advisor Cary Bazalgette
Production Assistance Caroline Elliston
Producer Michael Jackson

INTRODUCTION

This book, and the television series on which it is based, deal with popular, everyday television: soap operas, game shows, advertisements, the news, documentaries. Almost everyone watches these programmes: indeed, they are one of the most popular subjects of conversation. Tabloid newspaper articles relentlessly describe the lives of tv stars. But remarkably little serious attention is given to popular television. This book aims to go some way to redressing the balance.

Chapters One and Two of this book look at the viewers of television the first investigates metaphors used against viewers, the second looks at recent research into the part television actually plays in people's lives. Chapter Three investigates the prejudices against the most popular forms of television. Finally, the last two chapters look at some of the people who appear on television, as presenters of programmes, and as members of the public: 'real people' in television jargon.

In some ways it is strange to put a single author's name on the front of a book written in conjunction with a television series, where ideas emerge from group discussions. In this case, Michael Jackson, Paul Kerr, Gina Newson, Mike Dibb, Christopher Rawlence and Cary Bazalgette all contributed to the book in different ways, although I alone am to blame for the opinions (and for any mistakes). Since this book is intended as an introduction to some ways of looking at television, rather than a final word on the subject, I am also indebted to the work of many other writers. I hope most of these are listed in the bibliography at the back of the book. In addition, I would like to thank David Morley, who contributed far more than editors usually do, Jane Vaus, Jenny Boyce and Russell Southwood at Comedia and Jim Adams at the British Film Institute. Finally, thanks are also due to Paul Kerr and Steve Beresford, who both read the whole manuscript, Nic Gibson, Peter Moore, John Kieffer and George Gross.

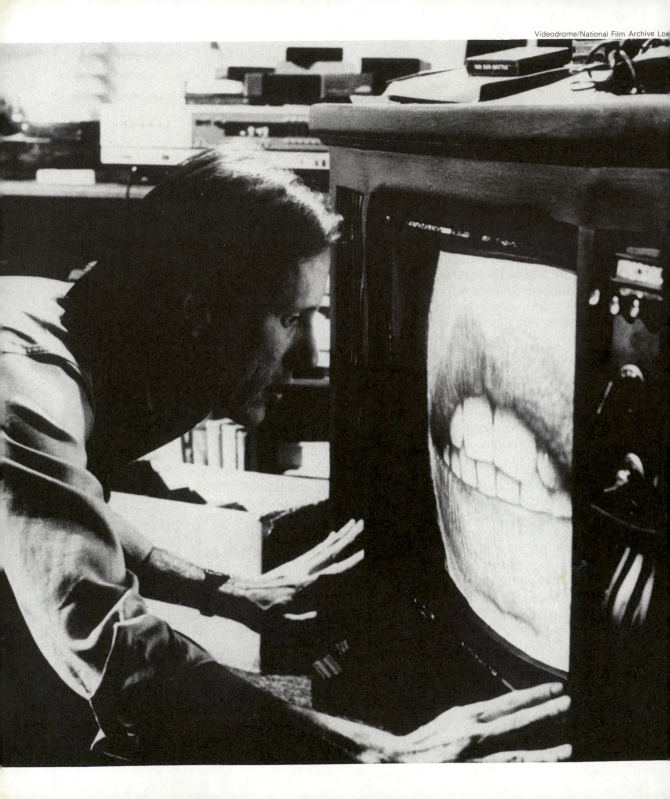

TELEVISION 1
ZOMBIES

The family is sitting in front of the TV, staring blankly at a fuzzy, low-quality image. Their eyes are glazed, their limbs hanging laxly from unhealthy bodies. Junk food is pushed mechanically into slackly open mouths. There is no conversation: just the occasional grunt as programme becomes advertisement and then becomes programme again.

This is one of the classic images of the television viewer, found in countless films, novels and comics. Cartoonists still use the TV zombie as the butt of innumerable jokes: heard the one about the man who watched the plug when the television went away for repair? Zombies also make frequent appearances in the snide columns of the 'quality' newspapers. It seems that some writers and critics are incapable of using the phrase '... in front of the television' without automatically adding the prefix 'slumped'. Sometimes, these characters show up on television itself – in serious plays like Mike Leigh's *Meantime*, or Lindsay Anderson's *The Old Boys*, and as the butt of jokes in sit-coms like *Till Death Us Do Part*, and *Hancock*. Even the BBC's children's programmes department called one of its productions *Why Don't You Turn Off The Television And Do Something More Interesting Instead?*

For a particularly memorable group of morons, turn to the youth movie. In the 'kitchen sink' drama *Saturday Night and Sunday Morning Morning* Arthur, the rebellious young working-class anti-hero, sneers at his father for doing nothing but 'watching the bloody telly day in, day out.' Twenty years later an almost identical scene appears in the chic, post-punk feature film *Repo Man*. Here, the wayward son watches horrified as his glassy-eyed parents are persuaded to part with all their money by a television evangelist. For 50's working-class rebels and seventies punks alike, zombified 'television parents' are a crucial metaphor for middle-aged malaise.

The best way to fight back against television? Kick in the set, of course. Accordingly, the destruction of a television has become an almost obligatory symbol of youthful anti-authoritarianism. The directors of pop promos use it, Video artists do it en masse. *Zabriskie Point*, the quintessential hippy rebellion movie, ends with a glorious display of exploding household appliances. Even David Niven, a most unlikely rebel, ends up putting his foot through the screen in *Happy Anniversary*.

According to these images viewers are characterless blobs who will watch anything – including, in some feature films, a blank, static-filled screen or the test card. Devoid of critical faculties, their relationship with television is shown as an involuntary physical reflex rather than a mental activity: they 'consume' a 'constant diet' of 'pre-digested fodder', 'lapping up' something which is 'churned out' from a 'sausage factory'.

If television is not junk food, then it is an 'anaesthetising' and 'addictive' narcotic: Marie Winn even called her stridently anti-television book about family viewing habits *The Plug-In Drug*. Large letters on its backpage blurb says it will 'help your children kick the TV habit.'

In much the same mode, an essay by *Evening Standard* TV-critic Milton Shulman was headlined 'The Big Fix'. From his perspective during 'the six neurotic weeks' leading up to the 1970 World Cup the BBC 'acted like some giant dope pedlar doing its best to fix the nation in some kind of psychedelic illusion'. And Hilary Kingsley of The *Sunday People* saw the fans of the soap opera *Crossroads* in a similar kind of way. During the 1979 ITV strike 'these were the ones with the worst symptoms of withdrawal pains. For them this four-times-a-week shot of soap opera had become as habit forming as a drug'.

Thought of like this, television is a sinister creation which has somehow found its way into the sitting rooms of the nation. And indeed, there is no shortage of evil televisions in science fiction films and books. *1984* shows the set as the agent of hidden state surveillance. *Hallowe'en Three* has a wicked toy manufacturer planning to infiltrate children's minds through advertisements. And in Stephen Spielberg's elegantly produced *Poltergeist* the TV set is the agent of the un-dead: after hypnotising a child with late-night static, it steals her away to the 'other side'. Television, it seems, is not so much part of family life, as a disturbing foreign force which has somehow managed to infiltrate our lives.

These sci-fi images of drugged and stupified television audiences can be paired with an opposite, but equally depressing, sister image. Curiously, as well as being glassy-eyed dupes, viewers are also often described in terms which make them sound like frantic, uncontrolled puppets. Members of this, second, group of automatons have a manic gleam in their eyes and a tendency to indulge in acts and beliefs which would never otherwise have

Happy Anniversary: **a classic cinematic attack on tv. Apparently an ultimate gentleman like David Niven can be turned into a thug by television.**

National Film Archive London

8

occurred to them. Apparently, at the same time as television makes us incapable of doing anything at all, it is also able to force us **to** do a whole series of things.

These frenzied zombies are manipulated by advertising into buying products they have no interest in and no use for. If we believe Vance Packard's **The Hidden Persuaders**, they arrive home from the supermarket loaded down with groceries purchased **solely** because of the 'spine-chilling' power of subliminal advertising. In his widely influential 50's book, Packard claimed that we respond to being 'treated like Pavlov's conditioned dog' with 'growing docility' and a propensity for 'impulsive and compulsive acts'. Rapists and murderers often use similarly inflated claims

National Film Archive London

about the power of media to excuse their behaviour. 'It was', some defence counsels like to say, 'television (or the film, or the video) that made him do it.'

Claims for the powers of television become particularly exaggerated when the audience is composed of children. Partly, this is because of the way we think about youth: in the west today we hold the myth of childhood as a 'golden age' very dear. We are not discouraged by the fact that this ideal is a fairly recent creation. Nor is this image affected by the astuteness which many children display about the world. As Cedric Cullingford says in an article on the effects of television, 'Children can understand the complexity of moral decisions by the age of five ... they can talk about the concept of thinking and the meaning of death between five and seven'. Despite this, Cullingford says we still tend to think of children as stupid or helpless when confronted with a TV set.

Since children are **supposed** to be innocent it becomes very useful to blame 'inappropriate' behaviour on some corrupting and devilish influence outside the family. Unsurprisingly, the alien 'box in the corner' comes high on many people's lists of bad influences.

The shocking combination of sweetly innocent children and devilishly influential television produces some of the most bizarre images of viewers as zombies. Television becomes something that actually causes an observable bodily reaction. In the fifties it was blamed for all manner of ailments from radiation sickness to crossed eyes. Buck teeth were also seen as the result of too much television: they were caused by sitting staring at the set with chin cupped on childish hands. For excessive imagery it is impossible not to quote Marie Winn's **The Plug-In Drug** even though it was written in the rather different context of American television. Using practically every phrase available in the zombie lexicon, she says 'the mental state of young children watching television is trancelike. The child's facial expression is transformed. The jaw is relaxed and hangs open slightly; the tongue rests on the front teeth (if there are any). The eyes have a glazed vacuous look.'

Like their parents, these children seem to manage to be simultaneously zombified and hyper-active: two states most people would regard as mutually exclusive. Later on in the same book, Marie Winn suggests that 'the frantic behaviour observed with greater frequency among children today' is partly the result of 'the frenetic over-stimulating pace of **Sesame Street** and other programs geared to pre-school children'. With offspring who manage to be at once frantic **and** vacuous it is hardly surprising that parents are worried.

THE SEETHING MASS

Marie Winn's theories find their most ardent supporters on the political right. Her nostalgia for an age of pre-televisual innocence, when children were children and women were content to stay in the kitchen, strikes a particular chord amongst those concerned about 'falling standards'. Obviously much of the left takes a rather different perspective on these developments. But this doesn't stop large sections from also believing the television viewer to be a gullible, stupefied dupe.

Their fear is not that television makes people into hyper-active hooligans: what haunts them is the spectre of people voting for Margaret Thatcher simply because **the television told them to do it**.

Apparently, they will do this whether voting Conservative is for, or against, their best interests, 'swallowing' pro-Thatcher messages on television without recourse to thought. Understandably, perhaps, this is an image with considerable appeal for the most beleaguered sections of the left. Expedient and resolute use of the strategy of 'blaming the media' allows them to skirt around complex and difficult problems. In particular, as a way of 'explaining' Thatcher's appeal it means that they can avoid the real issue – why many traditionally Labour voters now believe Tory policies offer an improved life for them and their children.

In fact, there is little evidence that political attitudes are formalised or altered in such direct ways. Writing about their famous and extensive research on the effects of television in the 1959 general election, the researchers Blumler and McQuail were forced to admit that 'within the frame of reference set up by our experiment, political change was neither related to the degree of exposure nor to any particular programme or argument put forward by the parties'.

Television is intertwined with politics in many complicated ways, but it does not make us suddenly switch political allegiance to a leader or party we would never otherwise have considered. As Ian Connell suggests, it is senseless to hurriedly ascribe 'fabulous powers' to the media, to believe that television can 'impose on *us*, win *our* acceptance of . . . entire ways of seeing and understanding quite outside of our everyday experience . . . If stories have been influential or persuasive, if they have consolidated particular interpretations, then it can only be because they have connected with feelings and thoughts that are already in place. The suggestion that these feelings and thoughts have simply been imposed on the audience by biased media is, really, little more than a convenient fiction'.

Predictably, the left version of the 'viewer as zombie' thesis also pays special attention to the manipulation of the young. Writing in a collection of essays about television and schoolchildren, Bob Ferguson says that 'there is a danger that programmes made for children can inhibit their capacity for thought and intellectual development'. Later on he suggests that 'There are, of course, certain young people who do reject the values implicit in the discourse of children's television. But their rebellion is often short-lived. The pull towards ideological containment via the smile of Terry Wogan or the inanity of many of the presenters of *Top of the Pops* is very strong.'

Ferguson's political alignment and areas of concern are poles apart from those of Marie Winn. He is worried about sexism and racism, while she is disturbed about the stability of the family. But

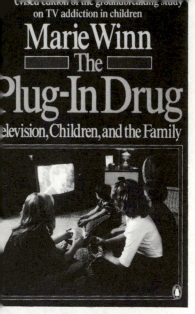

evised edition of the groundbreaking study on TV addiction in children

Marie Winn
The
Plug-In Drug
elevision, Children, and the Family

The Plug In Drug—**the addition metaphor becomes the title of a best-selling anti-television book.**

there are also similarities. Both dip into the standard anti-tv vocabulary, using the buzz-word 'vacuous' in their attempts to analyse the effects of too much viewing. She uses it for children's eyes; he has it describe the programmes they are watching. More dangerously, Winn and Ferguson are linked by the way they think of television viewing as a passive activity. Neither allows their young viewers much of a chance of independent thought or independent action. Zombified, they have little chance of escape.

It is revealing that neither Winn nor Ferguson think of themselves, or their own children as television zombies. Marie Winn's front-of-book biography proudly states 'The family owns a television set that is used for special occasions'. Accosted by the *Daily Mail*, Bob Ferguson's children said that they were anti-sexist and anti-racist, and never watched *Blue Peter*. 'We' never think of ourselves as driven to violence by television, see ourselves as gullibly accepting ill-fitting hand-me-down ideas or buying useless items. The zombies are always 'other people', those 'less able' to tell reality from fiction, those 'susceptible' to images of sex and violence. In the 60's obscenity trial brought against Penguin Books for publishing *Lady Chatterly's Lover*, an eminent lawyer claimed that he was not afraid of being corrupted by the book himself, but he was worried about what might happen if 'wives and servants' were allowed to read it. The same paternalistic logic lies behind arguments that viewers need to be protected from television 'for their own good'.

The theories of 'mass' behaviour developed in the nineteen thirties lump together the majority of (other) people as a faceless, collective throng. Created at a time when the rise of fascism badly needed explaining, they suggest that life in the twentieth century is fundamentally different from the experience of earlier generations. They claim that people have become isolated and powerless. Fragmented from older family structures, their working lives dominated by dehumanising industrialisation, individuals have become easy prey to manipulation by propaganda.

The theory impressed both the left and the right. Those on the right were concerned to account for the breakdown of old patterns of discipline and loyalty: the left, meanwhile, were interested in why parts of the working class had supported the Nazis, but did not seem ready for socialism. For left and right alike, however, they provided a philosophical basis for *investigating* the working classes – a group which they all tended to see as a fascinating, but alien, lifeform from another galaxy.

SEX 'N VIOLENCE

Images of 'mass society' were especially influential with the social scientists who were developing the 'effects' school of media research: a framework subscribed to by most anti-television writers. This crude approach explains the relationship between people and what they watch in ways of thinking borrowed from the natural sciences. Viewers are seen as a passive, inert mass which will always *respond* in a simple, observable way when presented with a *stimulus*. Television, it says, is like a drug: a one way process affecting those it is administered to in a similar and predictable manner. There is no room for thought or resistance and no space for the viewer to make creative use of television. In fact, the theory is often described as the 'hypodermic needle' model, since it proposes that ideas are *injectable* into a *subject* in much the same way that a chemical can be injected into a laboratory rat.

Strong traces of the hypodermic model can be seen in the cyclic panics about the effect of television violence, often blamed for so-called 'copy-cat' delinquency. To take just one example: David Mellor, a junior Conservative minister, recently declared to the House of Commons that 'violent films can give way to violent imitative behaviour'. He admitted that no-one had actually *proved* a link between television and youthful violence, but then claimed that 'common sense leads us to suspect that a constant diet (note the phrase) of violence ... can encourage repetition and encourage young people to engage in violence themselves'.

Just like some of the 'effects' scientists, Mellor and his parliamentary cohorts believe television and violent behaviour to be unproblematically and directly related. As related, in fact, as the convulsions of a laboratory animal and the poison that has just been administered to it. The child sees *Starsky and Hutch* pretend to hit someone; the child goes out and actually hits someone. A riot takes place on *The News*; teenagers watching plan one of their own.

Unfortunately for such campaigners, the idea of copy-cat violence flies in the face of all contemporary thinking about education which suggests that children *do not* learn by imitation. If they did, rote learning of Shakespeare would still be in use in a good many more schools. And *Blue Peter* would have had more success with its attempt to create 'a young nation of origami adepts, or dog handlers, or builders of lawn mowers out of coat hangers and wine corks', as novelist Ian McEwan neatly pointed out in The *Observer*.

The 'stimulus-response' theorists are unmoved by such ridicule.

'TV TO BLAME' FOR TINY TOTS VIOLENCE

By SARAH THOMPSON *Education Staff*

TELEVISION is largely to blame for class-room violence and disruptive behaviour, which have now spread to children aged only four and five, according to a new study.

Dr Jean Lawrence and her fellow lecturer at London University's Goldsmiths' College, Mr David Steed, interviewed the heads of 85 primary schools in 58 inner city areas and discovered 312 disruptive incidents caused by reception class infants in a single day.

The disruption, defined as action interfering with teaching or the running of the school, was starting among children three to five years younger than 10 years ago. They found:

A four-year-old who fought with his classmates constantly, causing minor injuries;

A five-year-old who would suddenly burst into prolonged, bizarre screaming fits, although normally quiet;

A five-year-old who pushed another's face into the coat pegs;

Another who punched a small girl in the stomach; and

An eight-year-old who kicked and punched a teacher after being told to squash berries into other children's hair.

Two other teachers had to be called to help out in this case.

In one inner city primary school, 28 disruptive incidents were recorded in one day. In all, boys started 79 per cent of the trouble.

Most disturbing

Lesser incidents included spitting, rolling on the floor and having fun with water in the lavatories.

adults from being figures of authority to figures of fun. Children used to come across very few adults before television. Now they saw hundreds a day.

The constant sight of adults being blown up and shot at did not enhance respect, said Dr Lawrence.

Close links

"Criminologists have got to be more interested in schools than they are now," she added. There were close links between disruptive behaviour in schools and delinquency later on.

"Every football hooligan has sat in a classroom at some time."

In their study nearby a third of the classroom incidents involved aggression, as opposed to inattentiveness or clowning. Mr Steed said yesterday: "Many of them seemed to be inept attempts at making friends and contact with their peers."

There was little vandalism, except in the case of one school whose head told the researchers that he could not fill in their questionnaire as his study had just been turned over by vandals from outside the school.

Parent contacts

Asked how best to cope with the problems, a third of the heads said that the most effective move was to improve con...

Borrowing more than metaphors from the science laboratory, they have spent a great deal of time and money attempting to test the 'effects' of televisual 'stimuli' in experimental conditions. Their usual routine is to deliberately place viewers in an alien environment: thereby, hopefully, eliminating the influence of friends, class attitudes, political affiliations, and so on. With all social factors apparently ruled out, the viewers are divided into groups and shown 'violent stimuli'. Subsequent behaviour is carefully charted. In some cases bodily changes such as blood pressures and sweating are tested with the aid of elaborate tools: for, just like Marie Winn, many experimenters are fascinated by the idea of television causing physiological variations.

The results of such tests, many of which claim to 'prove' that children respond violently after seeing images of aggression, have gathered spectacular amounts of publicity. Quotations from their findings are almost obligatory in anti-television campaigns: Marie Winn, Mary Whitehouse, the opponents of 'video-nasties' and clean-up tv campaigners like Winston Churchill all make references to them. And it is not only the right who have been attracted by these theories. Some feminist campaigns against male violence have swung dangerously close to backing the idea that images of violence are directly responsible for real violence. On closer examination, however, it looks like a shaky alliance: few effects researchers share the feminist's interest in social factors like male power, or economics.

Stalwart supporters of the 'effects' approach imagine the issue to be an open and shut case. Milton Shulman, for instance, believes the connection between television and violence to be as proved as that between 'smoking and lung cancer'. Others, however, are not so sure. Some opponents have suggested that these experiments are actually highly suspect, not least because of the difficulty of mimicking people's reactions in a laboratory. Experimental situations always create their own problems. The responses of the 'subjects' will often be warped by keenness to please the interviewer, just as schoolchildren expend ridiculous amounts of energy trying to second-guess what the teacher wants them to say. Asked if they enjoy violent television and videos, children often feel that they *should* say 'yes'. Sometimes they even admit to watching videos that don't exist. Many researchers use 'bobo' dolls: inflated three foot figures intended to act as the focus for the violent tendencies aroused by television. As she entered a laboratory, one small four year old girl was heard to say 'Look, Mummy, there's the doll we have to hit' ...

Another problem with effects research is its rather off-hand attitude to the 'violent stimuli' itself. Some researchers use feature

14

Biting the hand that feeds you. Newspapers are increasingly dependent on stories about television, but TV also provides an endless series of shock horror headlines.

DAILY EX

No. 23,869   Friday March 25 1977

Weather: Early fog; cloudy

TV shows 'danger to children'

Blamed: Starsky

Blamed: Hutch

THE VIOLENT HOUR

And the best of TV

Express Television Reporter **James Murray**

tele—

she complains, " conditions children to accept violence as an effective and necessary way of solving problems and ... their inhibitions about ...

I gave them a better offer says Heat

Express Staff Re

FORMER P Minister E Heath attack Liberals yes for their de Labour.

He said : " If going to be in ment you sho the responsibil is what gover all about."

His attack ca day after the Liberal leader kept Prime Mi Callaghan's Go power.

And it came after Mr. Heath to do a deal with In 1974 he o Liberal leader Thorpe a seat when the T General Electi He needed keep the Tori the offer was

Nati

Meanwhile smiled and through la version of B.B.C.'s N JOHN WAR Wearing a red Labo a Liberal o the Premier on monitor round the He drop and put p people wo

To a co people are dole than " I hope going to the gr his Bud He als tion for be down 1978. B next. horrid.

Predi on peop prices He c invited to his man— reveal letter about

The conqueror : Sian Phillips yesterday won a best actress award as Livia in " I Claudius." See Page 2

Daily Mail

THURSDAY, NOVEMBER 24, 1983   18p

FOUR WAYS TO WIN A MILLION SEE PAGE 34

EXCLUSIVE

Peace mission to halt arms race

From JOHN DICKIE in New Delhi

COMMONWEALTH it is being urged to a mission of four world s to Russia and the o urge an end to the ace. roposal is to ...

Videos replace baby sitters... and the children's party conjuror

Daily Mail Campaign

SADISM FOR SIX YEAR OLDS

BAN THE SADIST VIDEOS

films (*Rebel without a Cause* is a favourite) while others prefer cartoons, such as the infamous experiment which 'proved' that seeing an animated weed choke a flower made children more likely to burst a balloon. Behind such tests, is the belief that one violent moving image can stand in for the whole of television's violent output. The *Daily Mirror* made the same assumption in a special 'Sex and Violence on Our Screens' feature. It backed up its screaming assertion that 'Saturday night is bloodbath night on British television', with a headcount of nine murders on the national channels and 17 in the regions, 48 sex scenes and 4 rapes on one Saturday. They did not allow for the fact that the average Saturday schedule includes programmes as different as sit-coms,

December 16, 1985

The Sun

TV TO BLAME FOR CRIME WAVE, SAYS CHARLES

By TONY SNOW

Charles . . . "concerned about muggings of elderly"

PRINCE Charles believes TV sex and violence are partly to blame for the rising crime rate, a Tory MP said yesterday.

Geoffrey Dickens, who met the Prince at the weekend, said: "He was very concerned about the amount of violence on television.

'He feels it may be linked to crime, and I understand Princess Diana shares that view."

Mr Dickens said Charles told him at a London awards ceremony: "There are more TV sets than ever before, and more explicit productions." .

Mr Dickens — a leading campaigner against child abuse—said Charles asked him why that problem was "so dreadful."

Worried

And he said: "The Prince agreed when I said I thought it might be the result of sex and violence in our homes on TV."

Mr Dickens said: "He also told me he was dreadfully worried about the elderly being mugged in the streets."

HOME SECRETARY Douglas Hurd has called BBC and ITV chiefs to a special meeting tomorrow to discuss

documentaries, horror films, sport and serious drama: all of which can contain violent images. The journalists were after an inflated figure and for that one murder was as good as any other.

Dr. Belson falls into a similiar trap in his much discussed 'effects' book, *Television Violence and the Adolescent Boy*, which gives classification of the 'Violence Rating' of a whole series of programmes. *Yogi Bear* gets a rating of 1.42, *Steptoe and Son* 2.39, *Hawaii Five-O* 7.25, and *The Great War* 7.62. Incredible as it may sound, they assumed that the BBC's series on the mass slaughter of the 1st World War affected audiences in the same way as a light-hearted cop series. According to Belson, both play a part in inciting teenagers to delinquency and both should be censored.

But outside the laboratory, children know that programmes have distinct meanings, and are adept at recognising the distinct codes and rituals associated with separate parts of television. They understand the different meanings of car crashes on, say, The *A-team*, *Brookside* and The *News*. And they respond accordingly, realising that the noisy, stylised squealing of tyres in The *A-team* signifies fantasies of action, while the personalised violence of a soap opera is a signal for empathy and drama. And, equally, they know that news footage of a motorway pile-up means real death. Of course, a real cause for horror and confusion, would be the intrusion of the codes of the latter into one of the other forms: Mr T left dying and mutilated after a chase. But that, as any five year old knows, is impossible.

Strangely such commonplace knowledge evades the TV-violence lobby. They are fixated on the idea that children are diminutive zombies incapable of distinguishing between what is shown on television and what happens in the sitting room. But, as Ian McEwan says, 'The Kojak violence they witness is TV violence, sufficient to itself. It does not brutalise them to the point where they cannot grieve the loss of a pet stick insect, or be shocked by some minor playground violence. Children, like everyone else, know the difference between TV and life'.

The questions raised by doubtful experimental techniques and contradictory results are accompanied by the even bigger issue of whether the effects experimenters are asking the right questions. Alongside the studies that claim to conclusively prove a connection between television and violence there are others which suggest that there is very little relationship at all. To take just one example, a study compiled for the National Childrens Home found that 'a disturbed family relationship was a much more likely precursor of delinquency than was the act of television violence'. It is an amusing, if somewhat frightening, sign of the times that this commonsense platitude was regarded as worthy of a page three

17

report in The *Times*.

Few headlines proclaim that people most statistically likely to be violent watch least television. But, as Laurie Taylor and Bob Mullan say, 'there is no evidence whatsoever of members of the most violent age group in our society – sixteen to twenty-four – rushing home for their weekly fix' of The *Sweeney*, often berated as the most aggressive of British cop-shows. 'Quite the contrary. Television viewing in general is lowest amongst this age group and The *Sweeney* and other cops and robbers programmes do nothing to change this. In fact only 7% of those watching fall into this age group and they are out-numbered seven to one by those over fifty-five'. The appearance of the first laboratory experiments linking pensioners' viewing with subsequent violent acts are awaited with interest.

It is all very well for the American National Institute of Mental Health to say that 'TV is as strongly correlated with aggressive behaviour as any other behavioural variable that has been measured', but what exactly does that prove? As Joan Smith says, there is a huge 'chicken and egg problem' with this kind of finding. 'Studies have shown that aggressive adolescent boys are keener on violent programmes than non-aggressive boys. So do boys become violent because they watch violent television? Or do violent boys watch violent television because they enjoy it?'

And what about the 'variables' the effects researchers deliberately eliminate from their experiments? How is it possible to *measure* the impact of generations of deprivation? Or test the effects of racism in a laboratory? Or quantify the myth that violence is a 'natural' part of masculinity?

Television isn't blamelessly innocent of these unpleasant aspects of life, either. It is not simply 'there', a natural occurrence which can be taken for granted. But neither can it be detached from the rest of society. Television can't be understood by itself: it has to be seen as a *part* of the world, one element amongst the many that contribute to the delicate, complicated shape of social life.

It doesn't make sense to blame everything we happen to dislike on the influence of TV. But, just like the socialists who see television as responsible for the electorate's zombified acceptance of Margaret Thatcher, the clean-up tv campaigners are ready to accuse it of causing a vast array of 'social ills'. Copy-cat violence is only the beginning: the ever-lengthening list includes impolite behaviour, outlandish hairstyles, homosexuality, precocious female sexuality, loud music, all, apparently, the result of the evil box. The *Daily Mail's* Lynda Lee-Potter believes, for instance, that 'Children know only what we teach them and some television teaches that it's smart to be a rebel, clever to threaten and normal to be promiscuous.

To the historian these pronouncements may sound rather old-fashioned. And they are. The use of entertainment as a flamboyant scapegoat is not simply a phenomenon of the nineteen eighties. Before tv violence and video-nasties there were 50's horror comics, Hammer horror films, film-noir thrillers, and even melodramatic theatre. When John Gay's *The Beggars' Opera* was first performed in the eighteenth century it was accused of being responsible for an increase in highway robbery.

An editorial in an 1851 issue of the *Edinburgh Review* makes interesting reading in this context, especially when placed alongside Lynda Lee-Potter's article in the *Daily Mail* and others

National Film Archive London

In the Ealing comedy Meet Mr Lucifer **a failed actor meets the Devil and discovers television is his favourite toy: 'a mechanical device for making the human race utterly miserable'.**

like it. The editorial states that 'One powerful agent for the depraving of the boyish classes of our towns and cities is to be found in the cheap shows and theatres, which are so specially opened and arranged for the attraction and ensnaring of the young. When for 3d a boy can procure some hours of vivid enjoyment from exciting scenery, music and acting . . . it is not to be wondered that (he) . . . then becomes rapidly corrupted and demoralised, and seeks to be the doer of the infamies which have interested him as a spectator'.

Although divided by over a hundred years, the fears of the *Edinburgh Review* circa 1851, and the *Daily Mail* circa 1985 are almost identical. Seduced by moving images, the working class young will fail to show sufficient respect for their elders and betters. Chaos will prevail, if not revolution. It is not poverty and class bitterness, those old and entrenched tensions, which are the cause of the unrest, but theatre or comics or noisy television programmes. Get rid of the offending programmes they reassuringly tell their middle-class readers, and a whole range of awkward social problems will evaporate overnight.

Television, like all the other denounced popular forms that preceded it, becomes a whipping boy. 'Problems' from the breakdown of old patterns of family discipline, changing relations between the sexes, and the stroppyness of working class youth, are displaced onto it. In line with this, the programmes which suffer most badly from the campaigns of the tv-violence lobby are not always the most violent. Instead, they are those single plays, one-off documentaries and independent films which challenge established political orthodoxies. The film Mary Whitehouse actually brought a prosecution against (rather than simply attacking) was *Scum*, about borstal life, while two films by Derek Jarman, *Sebastiane* and *Jubilee*, bore the brunt of the attack in the second reading of the Obscene Publications (Amendment) Bill in the House of Commons. The discussion concentrated on their alleged violence: no-one seemed to have noticed that *Jubilee* was actually a surrealist punk fantasy. Beneath that, however, there were deeper worries about the films' sympathetic attitude to homosexuality. Is the spectre of 'TV violence' influencing zombies about to provide a smokescreen for a purge?

The first Radio Times television supplement. Television, it says is full of 'human interest' but the image is one of technology.

PART OF THE FURNITURE

If they are honest, most people can recall moments when it has been enjoyable to 'slump' in front of the television or even sleep in front of it. After a day of work or domestic stress it can be soothing to bask in the breathing space afforded by a half-watched programme – especially one we would otherwise regard as banal. Television can be very useful for blotting out the world and lulling us into a restful, uninvolved daze.

It can also be an effective means of insulating ourselves from other people and their demands. A parent suggesting that it is time for bed can be conveniently ignored with the help of a television set. And so can a friend or spouse who wants conversation when we don't feel prepared to give it.

The language of involuntary addiction and passivity is part of most people's everyday vocabulary for describing their viewing. We say we are 'hooked' on *Dallas* or *Juliet Bravo*. Often these words are used self-denigratingly when we are embarrassed to admit that we like a piece of television regarded as of unacceptably low status by our peer group.

These disdainful ways of talking about our viewing suggest that we don't all watch television in the same way throughout every evening. Instead, we use the set in different ways according to who we are and how we feel at a particular time. In one night, an individual may experience both the 'joys of slumping' *and* the pleasures of closely following a personal favourite.

Odd as it may sound, to think in this way about television involves a significant change of focus. It means accepting that television is *part* of life, rather than an alien influence casting a shadow over the family like a flying saucer in a sci-fi film. After all, it is only scientists studying effects and professional reviewers who watch television in a darkened room, insulated from the rest of the world. For the rest of us, tv watching goes on alongside the rest of our lives, counterpointing, illuminating, and occasionally disturbing.

Seen as an aspect of life, rather than as an isolated 'stimulus', television has greater possibilities than simply encouraging us to

be violent or to buy particular products. It has a role in defining what we think of as natural, suggesting, for example, that it is normal to laugh at certain things, that some attitudes are acceptable and others are beyond the pale. It helps, along with a whole series of other influences, to map out who we think we are, and what our place in the world potentially is. Countries we have never been to are given shape in our minds by television; attitudes we might not have encountered become plausible possibilities.

These grander frames of reference shift the emphasis away from paternalistic worries about how television affects 'other people'. Instead, we need to know what we make of television, and how it fits into our lives. The question about viewers becomes 'what they do with television', rather than what the box in the corner 'does to them'.

For the effects theorists television is a one way road. Power and influence flow in a single direction: *from* the mind-numbing set *to* the slumped, passive viewer. Recent research into television makes the process into a two way street, with viewers actively working to make sense of what they see. Instead of being manipulated zombies, they become a vital part of the whole experience of watching television. An evening with the television becomes an evening doing something, not time spent in a trance-like stupor.

For a start, years of armchair criticism have given most viewers a complex, if not very theoretical, vocabulary for assessing actors performance, presentation, period detail, underlying political attitudes and the potential pleasures of any programme. The majority of viewers have a good idea when a programme is succeeding within it's own terms: that applies whether the programme in question happens to be **Who Dares Wins**, **World in Action** or **Deadhead**. Viewers can also recognise a dud which doesn't work for them: very few are sloths when it comes to identifying an arid or confusing documentary, an unfunny sit-com, or a music programme with last months bands. They might find it hard to define, but viewers are highly skilled in isolating programmes which deliver what they are looking for.

The extensive knowledge of plot detail possessed by some viewers would credit a professional archivist: witness the niggling letters which flood in whenever a long-running series makes a continuity error. This detail can also offer less finicky pleasures. Charlotte Brunsdon, for example, has described how 'skilled soap opera viewers' get the most out of serials. Using their knowledge of previous episodes, an experienced viewer can predict what might happen to a particular character. They might well lay a bet, for instance, that no romance started by **Coronation Street's** brassy bar-maid Bet Lynch is ever likely to culminate in wedding bells.

Real fans will also have insights culled from an understanding of the conventions of soap opera in general. They would know, for instance, that marriages run into trouble more frequently than those in real life, and that within the world of soap opera far fewer pregnancies result in live births. Every regular soap viewer appreciates that a casual mention of an adoption will, sooner or later, result in an appearance of the lost child. Indeed, as Charlotte Brunsdon says, 'For the soap fan, one of the moments of pleasure is when you can say "Oh, I *knew* that was going to happen".'

Keen viewers will get a further priming from reading the tabloids, which now cover the soaps with an almost obsessive ardour. Information gleaned in this manner can, with careful application, provide a whole additional dimension to the programmes. Tit-bits about the real-life situations of various stars are particularly important: most regular viewers of *Dallas* knew that actor Patrick Duffy was planning to leave the series long before Bobby Ewing had his fatal head-on collision with Katherine's car. In the same way, viewers will also know about plot developments influenced by industrial changes at the television companies. After producer Philip Bowman took over *Crossroads* many regular viewers worried every time a favourite character was shown with a cold, or going on holiday. Would they return to continue in the series? Or had Bowman, dubbed 'the axeman' by some of the tabloids, decided to get rid of them permanently?

Armed with such information and bolstered by the everyday skills of being able to judge situations and weigh up people, the viewer can predict what is likely to happen: who a new character will team up with, for example, or how a particular storyline will end. But, as Charlotte Brunsdon points out, no viewer, however experienced, can tell exactly *how* the development will take place. What will the fatal accident actually be? Where will it take place? How will other characters react? There, of course, lies the enjoyment.

Soap opera is not the only type of television where an understanding of the conventions contributes to the pleasure. The more familiar a viewer is with a situation comedy, for instance, the greater the potential enjoyment from seeing the internal rules in operation. Regular *Minder* viewers all appreciate that the newest Arthur Daley scheme will somehow collapse: it is the anticipation of the event through the twists and turns of the plots which is delightful. We *know* Arthur will find somewhere else to be when a situation gets 'physical', just as we expect Tel will blunder, good-heartedly, into trouble if he helps the woman he thinks is a damsel in distress. What we can't guess, are the specifics. Arthur, as all fans know, has a hundred places to hide, Terry, a thousand ways to come a cropper. The pleasure for us is seeing the precise

interaction between the things we know will happen, and the elements we can never predict.

'Effects' scientists imagine viewers to be identical, easily-persuaded members of a faceless mass. But, as we all know from experience, people's actual lives are far too untidy to be shoehorned into the neat family groups on the covers of the anti-television books. We rarely even gather in front of the set like that. Interviews with London families carried out by David Morley lead him to say that 'it is a most unlikely occurrence for everyone to spend the evening sitting down watching television together. It's far more common for different people to be watching television at different times – and wanting to see different programmes'. Multi-set ownership has made this desire possible: according to the latest figures published by the IBA a majority of households with children now have two sets.

Individual family members will usually have quite separate ways of viewing the same programmes. **Top of the Pops** will not be experienced in the same way by an enthusiastic nine-year old and her grandad who watches the dancers but complains about the noise: arguably, both have their own ways of enjoying the programme. Other viewers employ the camp, ironic attitude used by Nancy Banks-Smith when she says 'I am addicted to **Crossroads** (ATV) not for its virtues, which escape me at the moment, but for its faults. I love it because of its warts, as it were. An infatuation based on faults is difficult to cure . . .' Watching television like this allows the viewer both a 'cool' distance from the programme **and** the luxury of concentrated viewing: useful for someone worried about being identified as 'the type of person who watches **Crossroads**'.

This new perspective suggests that how we understand a programme depends on who we are. It sees viewers as people with social lives and domestic habits, likes and dislikes. They gain a gender and a sexual preference, a class, a race and even, perhaps, imagination and a sense of irony: attributes unimaginable in the slumped, passive hoards. Viewers bring their social and political identity with them to the television set. Research by David Morley on the audience for **Nationwide** and by Justin Lewis into **News at Ten** suggests that the framework viewers slot programmes into are all-important in determining how they 'read' an item. Some **Nationwide** viewers, for instance, thought the show was danger-ously biased towards the left, while others felt it represented the establishment through and through.

Findings of this kind involve a dramatic shift away from the ideas of the effects theorists. For them, television programmes were simple, easily-transmitted messages, which meant exactly the

24

same to everyone who watched them. For writers like Brunsdon, Morley and Lewis, the meaning of a programme depends on who the viewer is and which 'method' of watching they are using. This does not mean, however, that viewers have complete freedom to make just *any* interpretation of the programme at will. As Justin Lewis says, 'It is not a case of the viewer choosing on the basis of his or her predilections which part of the message he or she feels is important and then constructing a suitable meaning'. The options open to people are limited by who they are and how they understand the world. At any given time, only a limited number of interpretations of a situation are conceivable possibilities: the rest are simply beyond our grasp. We cannot simply slip out of ourselves and choose to see everything through somebody else's eyes, however much we might want to do so.

Our understanding also tends to be constrained by the nature of television itself. Viewers do not have *as much* power as the broadcasting institutions who produce what we see. Each programme comes ready packed with what has been called a 'preferred reading': a set of interpretations provided by the producers. For instance, a statement read over a still photograph will guide us towards a particular way of 'reading' the image. A news item which describes a man with a gun as a 'terrorist' is pushing us to react differently to one which describes him as a 'guerilla'. The reception given to a piece of television drama will be limited by the ways in which it is discussed and scheduled: people will be primed to react in a different way if it appears in early evening primetime, or in a more prestigous single play slot. But, despite these pressures, we are not actually forced to accept the 'preferred reading', just as we are not actually forced to watch at all.

PAYING ATTENTION?

The soundness of these new approaches has been graphically demonstrated by some experiments which used television to *watch the viewer*. Peter Collett, a psychologist at Oxford University, placed a cabinet containing an ordinary television, a video camera, a microphone and a timing device in the living rooms of 20 different families for a week each.

The most startling thing about the resulting videos is the variety of ways in which we watch television. A minority of viewers are passively slumped in front of their tvs. Many are 'absolutely locked into what is happening on the screen', in Collett's words. And, another, almost equally large number, appear to be oblivious to the fact that the television is on at all. People engage in an almost

Peter Collett

Peter Collett

Not everyone sits slumped like a zombie. Peter Collett's experiments 'watching people watching television' with the aid of a video camera found that people do a whole range of things in front of the set. In these stills from his videos the main pictures show what happens in viewers' living rooms, while the inset boxes show the picture on television at the time.

bizarre variety of different activities in front of the set: we eat dinner, knit jumpers, argue with each other, listen to music, read books, do our homework, kiss, write letters and vacuum-clean the carpet. According to Collett, 'People spend hours on end doing all kinds of things that have absolutely nothing to do with TV viewing while the set is on'. It would be strange if we didn't. As Dr Robert Towler, head of research at the Independent Broadcasting Authority, says, 'The TV moguls are so busy saying how wonderful it is that viewing has gone up to 32 hours a week, they fail to notice that people simply can't be *watching* that amount unless they suspend their daily lives altogether'.

Evidence from the diaries kept by members of the Mass Observation movement suggest that these ways of using television are comparatively new. During the fifties it was far more common to sit in absolute silence. One woman's account of watching The *Coronation*, (her first encounter with television) records that the group 'did not talk much during the day as we were too absorbed in watching, and, for most of the time quite unaware of our surroundings'. The extent to which that has changed is illuminated by a woman interviewed in a recent report by the D'Arcy Masius Benton Bowles advertising agency. She says, 'When television first came out you'd go to call on somebody and they'd say "hush, we're watching so and so". Nobody does that nowadays'.

According to David Morley's interviews men and women tend to watch television in very distinct ways. Men, he says, 'state a clear preference for viewing attentively, in silence, without interruption, in order not to miss anything'. Women, however, tend to think of television as a social activity and will happily try to continue conversations while viewing. In fact, these male and female approaches to television are so different that Morley notes many 'men display puzzlement at the way their wives and daughters watch tv.' In some cases their contrary approaches to viewing seem to be the source of considerable tension: several of the women said their husbands 'are always on at them to shut up'.

For many women, to *just* watch television would be regarded as an 'indefensible waste of time'. 'Women are', David Morley says, 'very conscious of their domestic obligations. While watching the tv they are ironing, or knitting, or sewing, or keeping an eye on the other needs of the family.' Women, it seems, simply don't have the time to watch television attentively – a fact grimly supported by figures which show that while the majority of women now have jobs outside the home, they are still responsible for almost all the housework.

That we are doing other things in front of the set doesn't necessarily mean that we aren't taking in anything from the programmes. Everyday experience tells us that it is quite possible to keep an eye on a meal and watch the news, or even to stand in the kitchen and follow a drama showing in the living room from what is said on the soundtrack. This, apparently, is how the Pain family managed to learn enough about television to slaughter all-comers in the BBC's *Telly Addicts* competition. Chrissie Pain, the mother, told The *Radio Times* that 'I don't know how we know so much really ... There's no moment when we drop everything to watch the box. I'm more often knitting or reading and in the summer I'm always working in the garden. Glen sort of potters and I often find Adi sound asleep upstairs in front of her portable.'

Many television programmes are deliberately designed to allow us to watch television while also getting on with the rest of our lives. Frank Bough, ex-presenter of *Nationwide*, was happy to admit that people didn't watch in a concentrated fashion. He says in his autobiography *Cue Frank!*, that 'The time of the day we appear is a very busy time of day for a great many people . . . who are only just arriving home, saying hello to the children, preparing meals, feeding babies. The format of *Nationwide* is such that you can pause for a minute or two to watch an item that interests you or catches the attention, and then return to what you are doing. Ours is not necessarily a time of day when people are ready to sit and give their undivided attention to an in-depth conversation on the economic state of the nation . . . The magazine style is unbeatable at that time of the evening'.

This pattern has become an almost obligatory feature of early evening non-fiction programmes. *Nationwide*, itself modelled on the magazine programme *Tonight*, was followed on the BBC by *60 Minutes* and *Wogan*, all of which have a fast moving, compartmentalised form. The same goes for the local news programmes which shape the early evening schedules of the independent companies.

In his book *Visible Fictions*, John Ellis suggests that this segmented form is the characteristic shape of all television, whether it is a news or magazine programme item, a title sequence, a group of advertisements or even a dramatic scene in a police show or soap opera. The segments each make sense by themselves: we can catch a quick, compartmentalised unit, do something else, come back to another unit and still understand what is going on. Hardly the stereotyped image of the family 'glued to the set': in fact, it could even be seen as a rather skilled way of watching.

John Ellis is rather dismissive when he says that television only requires 'short bursts of attention'. For him, the intense commitment to long-term viewing demanded by feature films is a superior and more challenging experience. The luxurious self-involvement of watching a film in a cinema is, however, light years away from the chaotic scramble of most sitting rooms between 6.00 and 8.00 pm. For a television drama to have meaning, its audience needs to be able to follow what is going on. Very early evening soap operas, particularly *Crossroads* and *Emmerdale Farm,* are distinguished by short scenes and almost obsessive repetition of plot elements. When, for instance, *Crossroads* introduced Martin Smith, a new character with a potential drink problem, his weakness was underlined by an almost endless succession of loudly demanded doubles. New actors can find this a mystifying process: in a *Time*

Out article Geoff Brown noted that 'performers new to the genre sometimes interrupt rehearsals to complain, I've **said** that!' But, they say it again and again, until the plotline has spent itself'.

To the viewer giving *Crossroads* careful attention, this may be seen as a sign of crassness and dramatic ineptitude. But to the woman trying to watch at 6.30 while she feeds the family, it is this reiteration which makes it watchable. Sandra Smith, a regular viewer who watches with her five children says 'It's not too much of a speedy programme. If you do miss something, you'll not miss too much. Now, a lot of people don't like that, they say it's too slow. But for me, it helps when they repeat things. I need those little quirks.'

THE TELEVISION EXPERIENCE

As well as struggling to concentrate through the filter of family activities, most of us are also familiar with a rather different strategy for using television: keeping the set switched on, without even **trying** to take in anything on the screen. Few people, however, employ only this method. It is far more common for viewers to switch rapidly back and forth between different modes of watching – at one point concentrating intensely, at another using the television as a kind of background music.

When television is kept on continuously it becomes a kind of 'filler' behind conversations and domestic events. Used like this, television is not so much a series of individual, contrasting programmes, as a constant presence inhabiting the sitting room. In many houses, it is so habitual a part of family life that the act of turning off the set signifies a major family confrontation or tragedy.

As well as a form of electronic communication, television can be part of the fittings of a room. It becomes a device for gently altering mood, by providing sound, colour and movement, or a source of domestic comfort in the same way as a fire, or a radio. This is what people are seeking when they turn on the television as they go into a dark house, along with the lights and fire.

And it is, after all, 'the experience' of television that we purchase. When we pay for our license fee, we are 'buying' everything on television, not just the programmes we want to see, like the specific films we choose to pay for at the cinema.

Another approach to television as a 'whole experience' comes from Raymond Williams, one of the first university academics to look seriously at how we watch television. In his book *Television, Technology and Cultural Form* Williams says it is significant we often say 'we have been "watching television" rather than that we

have watched "the news" or "a play" or "the football".' When we sit in front of the set we aren't so much taking in distinct, separable 'items' as basking in a continuous, interwoven 'flow' of sounds and images. As we sit, programmes merge into other programmes and mingle with advertisements, trailers and channel announcements, resulting in a confusing, amorphous collage. An evening spent with the television is, he says, 'like having read two plays, three newspapers, three or four magazines on the same day that one has been to a variety show and a lecture and a football match. And yet in another way it is not like that at all, for though the items may be various the television experience has in some important effect unified them'.

As Raymond Williams points out, most newspaper critics haven't yet come close to dealing with this question. Instead of trying to approach the slippery issues raised by thinking about the 'experience' of television, they tend to take the easy way out and break 'the flow' up into neat, reviewable units. What is required, Williams implies, is a new language to describe television. We need categories helpful for thinking about how we **watch** television, rather than ones created inside the television industry to answer a different set of problems. For instance, there should be a phrase to talk about the parts of television where the commercial breaks are an essential part of the overall effect. This could be used to describe The *Tube and* the pop-promo style record adverts that are interspersed throughout it. Perhaps there should also be a term to specify the hidden bits of television: the continuity announcements, channel identifications, and 'menus' which tell us what is coming up next. None of these get listed in the Radio or TV Times, but they are a vital part of the experience of watching television.

The concept of 'flow' is a step in the right direction, but Williams uses it in a way which is dangerously close to the pessimism of the effects theorists. Basing many of his comments on a fraught and exhausting confrontation with American broadcasting, he says flow turns tv into a confusing and rather depressing experience. Everything is reduced to a muddied sameness, rather like Plasticine which has been played with for too long. And the viewers? Although he includes himself in this category, Williams' viewers have more than a passing similarity to our old friends the slumped, passive zombies. 'It is widely, if ruefully admitted . . .' he says ' that many of us find television very difficult to switch off; that again and again, even when we have switched on for a particular "programme" we find ourselves watching the one after it and the one after that'. We may like to deny that we 'just sit there hour after hour goggling at the box', but 'the fact is that many of us do sit there

and much of the critical significance of television must be related to this fact.'

This rather melancholy image doesn't match up with the way most of us encounter tv. These days, a different kind of 'viewer controlled' flow is possible with the aid of the remote control which allows us to zap back and forward between channels, avoiding disliked parts of programmes – or the commercials, as the advertising agencies have nervously noted. Some viewers are, in fact, deliberately exaggerating 'flow' by rapidly switching channel: hardly a passive experience. Especially skilled viewers can even keep an eye on two different programmes at once: an ability which will be further tested by soon-to-be-marketed sets which allow viewers to 'taste' other channels through a small box inserted in the main picture.

Aside from idle fiddling, most people use remote controls to change channel in order to see an individual programme. For despite Raymond Williams' vision of us stuck 'goggling at the box', unable to summon up the energy to switch station, most of us have very definite programme favourites which we will change channels to watch. According to Sue Stoessl, head of marketing at Channel 4, the willingness to change channels is increasing. 'People move around more than they used to. Partly that's the result of remote controls, but it is also because the existence of minority channels has forced them to. Part of the "shock horror" response when Channel 4 began was because viewers didn't pick and choose. It was a commercial station, so they stuck with it and came across things that were just horrific to them. Now they look through the listings and find programmes that appeal.'

Video is also increasing the choice available to viewers: David Morley's research suggests that it is increasing the tendency of individual family members to use the television in their own particular ways. 'Some teenagers organise their social lives around video, inviting their friends round to watch their videos and then going to friends' houses to see other tapes. In the same way, some women invite friends round to watch tapes of favourite fictional programmes. In particular, they do this when their husbands and sons are out of the way; they feel, they enjoy the programmes more in the company of other women who like the material in the same way that they do.'

Findings like these suggest that unless television offers the experience we are looking for, we turn off, or over, or concentrate on something else while leaving the set on. Paul Fox, Managing Director of Yorkshire Television, comments that 'One of the most impressive things about the audience is their rejection rate. There are comedy programmes which start with an audience of say 10

million, because the star and the story are attractive and the ballyhoo which has gone on before has encouraged them to watch. But, by golly, they will then reject it quickly if they don't like it. By week two that audience will have been reduced by 20 or 30%, with another 10% going the next week.' And Peter Collett says, 'People are not slaves to the medium of television in that they exercise an enormous degree of choice over the programmes they watch. When it comes to tv they are masters of their own fate.'

The mere existence of ratings battles helps to prove the strength of viewers' preferences. The BARB ratings, based on electronic diaries of viewing kept by 2,500 households, are the 'currency' of the television industry. Although primarily geared at the advertisers and used to peg the price of advertising 'slots' (the more viewers of the right sex, class, etc, the greater the cost of the time), the ratings are also regarded as a general, numerical gauge of the success of a programme. Partly because of this, the ratings are bickered about throughout the industry. Some producers, whose programmes get lower figures than they think they deserve, are perturbed by the 'missing millions', those who time-shift with their videos or tune their televisions through their video recorder. Others, particularly those working for Granada's **Coronation Street**, dispute the new system of adding the figures from the weekend 'omnibus' editions of **EastEnders** and **Brookside** into their overall weekly audience scores – a change which helped **EastEnders** push **Coronation Street** out of its time honoured place at the top of the ratings.

These wrangles make entertaining journalism, and give tabloid readers a fascinating insight into how the television industry thinks about them, the viewers. (Interestingly, the 'heavy' papers are not nearly so concerned.) But, as data which are heavily relied on by some tv professionals, the ratings say remarkably little about how people actually watch television. Counting how many people are in their sitting rooms with their tv's switched on tells us nothing about how they are watching: they might, after all, be watching in an ironic way, turning over to ridicule and sneer. Or, as the Peter Collett tapes suggest, they might just happen to be in the same room and not be paying the slightest attention to the television.

The ratings show that people are selective in their choice of channel, but that is as far as it goes. In their current form, the ratings have a very limited view of the options available to the viewer. People can push buttons and turn programmes on and off, but as far as BARB is concerned that is all that viewers are capable of. BARB is not interested in the myriad uses people make of individual television programmes, or in the 'work' audiences contribute to viewing their favourite programmes. Instead, the

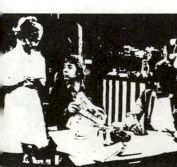

ratings' purpose is to obsessively count heads: a technique vaguely reminiscent of the work of Dr. Belson and other effects scientists. As in his studies, it is the statistical correlation of numbers of viewers with events that matters, not the nature of their experience with television.

BARB backs up the numerical ratings data with a survey of attitudes called the appreciation index (or AI), but within the industry, these AI's do not, on the whole, exert the powerful influence of the ratings proper. Certainly, it is the simple 'headcounting' approach to audiences which has traditionally dominated the outlook of those who buy and sell television time. These days, however, those on both sides of the counter are paying increasing attention to the more complex sections of BARB which illuminate the detail of who audiences are. Rather than marketing departments simply trying to 'deliver' the largest possible general audience, they are starting to divide their audiences into small target groups. Looked at this way, minority programmes start to look like a very good bargain. For instance, the audience for American football is overwhelmingly biased towards young male viewers, a group usually considered difficult for television advertisers to reach because of the small amount of television they watch. Their spending power is turning American football into a prime site for commercials selling jeans, beer and cars.

In the future, some elements of the advertising industry may move even further away from a numerical approach. Sue Stoessl, for instance, says that future research could hinge on whether people pay more, or less attention, to a commercial when it occurs during a programme they are deeply involved in. In her view people are more likely to be attentive if they are keenly awaiting the next instalment, an attitude which contradicts the traditional wisdom that people's irritation with the interruption will rub off on the products.

Still to be integrated into the advertising industry's attitude to viewers is the fact that people make definite choices about advertising. Peter Collett's tapes show that viewers don't sit passively 'lapping up the messages', as some in both pro and anti-advertising camps tend to assume. As Peter Collett says, 'It's not the case that people remain rivetted to the tv set during the breaks. Some get up, some make coffee, a lot of people zap to another programme, a lot of people yawn.'

Not everyone responds in this way, though: the tapes reveal some people zapping *into* commercials. Steve and Mary Griffiths, one of the couples 'spyed on' by Collett's machine, say 'we will quite consciously sit and watch the commercials to see if there is a favourite one, and then turn over onto another channel. Most of

them are awful, but there are a handful which are entertaining: we wait for them.' The seductive visual glamour produced by the vast amounts of money lavished on some commercials is undoubtedly partly responsible for this affection, as is the growth of comedy commercials. But, the fact that certain images are enjoyed, does not automatically give them the power to influence purchases. The famed Leonard Rossiter/Joan Collins commercials may have entered folk mythology, and done wonders for the careers of both stars, but the current feeling in the advertising industry was that they did little for Cinzano. Or was it Campari?

TV AND EMOTION

Television professionals should not be too disturbed by Collett's revelation that people are talking, eating and kissing their way through carefully produced programmes. The flip-side to this seeming inattention is that these same people often feel very strongly about television. They experience accute disappointment when they miss episodes of their favourite series, they collect video tapes and buy TV-related ephemera. But, even deeper than that, many people have a highly emotional involvement with television. Being a viewer can be an intense experience: one which makes us laugh, moves us, and with surprising frequency, makes us cry.

Going by letters to newspapers and by the evidence of Peter Collett's tapes, it is common for viewers to have powerful, emotive responses to programmes, be they *World in Action*, *Edge of Darkness* or *EastEnders*. Television, the viewers say, is a moving experience: a response very different from the arid vision conjured up by American author Jim Trelease. 'Television', he says, 'has encouraged our society to speak less, feel less and imagine less'. It is interesting to contrast his tone with that of a letter to the *Radio Times* from a Manchester woman about *Tender is the Night*: 'I wish I had words to convey the depth of pleasure - the pleasure of recognition - that this beautiful production brought to me. My 16 year old daughter, very up-to-date in her ideas about life, was in tears at the end'.

In a similar vein, Laurie Taylor comments on the surprising number of men in his research groups who admitted crying over soap operas. The members of one group talked about *Coronation Street* in this way:

> 'Alan (37): Well, Ken and Deirdre, when they were having that bust-up, that was so emotional. It was good TV. It choked you up a bit.
> John (44): It was saddest, though, when she went back to him.

Alan: Yes.

John: Yes, I reckon she should have left him.

Dennis (49): I sometimes get sad about Hilda. She gets put upon. Sometimes Hilda gets put upon.

Dennis: I must be perfectly honest, I watched it when Stan died, I watched it and cried. I sat down and watched it when Stan died because it was so real and I could relate to it. I just sat there and cried.'

Comparable feelings are part of many people's everyday experience of television. Television events like *Live Aid*, and documentaries like *Alice, A Fight for Life* and plays like *Cathy Come Home* all work by engaging our sentiments. So, in different ways, do 'happy' non-fiction programmes like *This is Your Life* and *Surprise, Surprise.* It is almost impossible to discuss the *EastEnders*' cot death, Fallon's funeral in *Dynasty* or *Boys From the Blackstuff*, without someone talking in an emotional way.

Sometimes there will be a clear connection between what is shown in a programme and experiences in the rest of our lives: we may cry over a documentary for example, because it reminds us of a similar situation. But that is comparatively rare. The majority of people who mourned the death of Bobby Ewing were not remembering road accidents.

Much more usually, the emotion comes from a sensuous (and sometimes rather masochistic) interaction between 'tragic' television and the viewers' own complex imaginative lives. Melodramas like *Dallas* where *everyone* is unhappy, despite their wealth, power and beauty, exert a powerful allure, especially when the programmes' direct emotional appeal is allied with a lush visual style. Alongside the astounding impact of the glossy prime-time soaps, there has been a parallel tendency for pain-filled films to dominate factual television. The sixties saw the rise of emotional documentaries like *Man Alive*, *This Week* and *People in Trouble*, and drama-documentaries such as *Cathy Come Home*, still remembered in detail by a surprising number of viewers. The eighties, meanwhile, have been characterised by intimate, small-scale films, such as those regularly seen on *40 Minutes* and *First Tuesday*. In fiction and non-fiction alike, some of the most resonant and popular programmes seem to be those with an explicit emotional appeal.

Oddly, few researchers have commented on this characteristic of television, or asked how it affects the viewer's relationship with the medium. The blame for this peculiar oversight, as Laurie Taylor and Bob Mullan have suggested, probably lies in the academic and tabloid obsession with television as a cause of

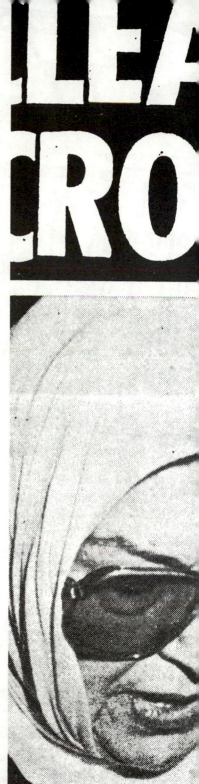

DAILY STAR

TUESDAY, JUNE 23rd, 1981   10p   (12p C.I.s, 15p Eire)   Printed in London

CONFESSIONS OF MEG
CENTRE PAGES

10p AS USUAL

Brat serves up a cussin match

By JAMES WHITAKER

SUPERBRAT John McEnroe came within an ace of cussing himself out of Wimbledon yesterday.

The No. 2 seed's temper matched the blistering 80s temperature as he earned himself two penalty points for insulting both the umpire and the tournament referee.

He called umpire Edward James, an "incompetent fool" and swore at referee Fred Hoyle.

Earlier, the abrasive young American had received a public warning for jumping on his racquet and smashing it.

Outbursts

Referee Hoyle confirmed last night that under Grand Prix rules McEnroe was only two steps away from forfeiture of the match and exit from the championship.

McEnroe, whose outbursts were watched by his father from the stands, went on to defeat fellow American Tom Gullikson.

Meanwhile, that other bad man of tennis, Ilie Nastase, went down cursing, kicking and clowning to American Sandy Mayer.

At one stage he called the umpire a "son of a bitch."

Duchess's agony : Page 4
Wimbledon : Back Page

CLEAROUT AT CROSSROADS

A shattered-looking Noele Gordon yesterday   Picture: DAVE ADAM

TV's CROSSROADS is itself at the crossroads.

And Noele Gordon's sacking is just the start of wholesale changes in the 17-year-old show.

More stars of the hit soap opera face the heave-ho before the end of the year as ATV bosses try to make the serial less middle-class and less middle-aged.

Lovable chump

Housewives' heart-throb Ronald Allen, who plays motel boss David Hunter, may be the next to go.

His screen son, Chris, played by Stephen Hoye, and waitress Diane Hunter (Sue Hanson) are also likely to be axed.

And even that lovable chump Bennie, played by Paul Henry, is thought to have outlived his usefulness.

ATV programme controller Charles Denton and new drama boss Margaret Matheson have decided on a new policy for the Eighties.

Develop

"They think the show is old-fashioned," said one member of the Crossroads team.

"At the moment, one idea is to have a major disaster at the motel — a fire and an explosion are being considered.

"Then they can kill off who they like and rebuild the serial at the same time as the motel."

Mr. Denton said : "We

Noele just the first to get the motel axe

By STAFFORD HILDRED

have to bring in some new blood and point Crossroads in a new direction.

"It will change and develop but the viewers will have to wait and see how.

"I wish I had had the chance to tell Noele Gordon of the decision, and it is my decision, but she has refused to see me.

"In any case there is no chance of it being altered."

Miss Matheson, who took over as controller of drama two months ago refused yesterday

to discuss specific characters.

But she did say : "Inevitably new characters will come into Crossroads and some of the more long established longrunning ones will drop out."

Shocks

Of Noele Gordon's sacking she commented: "Life is full of shocks.

Miss Gordon understood to have made a personal appeal to save her job to Lord Grade, chairman of ATV's parent company Associated Communications Corporation.

But the sacking of

Turn to Page

TURN TO PAGE 16 AND CATCH UP NOW ON THE £30,000 TRAIL

The ★ DAILY STAR

TODAY, the giant Mecca chain join the ever-growing army of Star Super Bingo players. For at Mecca's 139 Social Clubs throughout Britain, Star Bingo cards are being distributed free.

That means you can join the £30,000 treasure trail today (and we've reprinted the first two days' numbers just to make sure you don't miss the action).

And don't forget there's an extra £20,000 to be won every week in the Star Cash Bonanza—get your leaflet and/or your Bingo card at your newsagents' now !

He'll be happy to serve you, for there's £1,000 in it for him if you're a winner PLUS £250 for the newsboy or newsgirl who delivers the winning Star.

Yes, folks, there are chances for everybody in the great Bingo Bonanza giveaway !

violence. Beside the desperate (and highly-funded) search to find a 'reason' for crime, the vast amounts of everyday tears shed for Bobby Ewing and his like probably look insignificant. Moreover, to achieve anything, such an investigation would have to ditch prejudices about the passive similarity of 'the mass' of viewers. How else could a researcher tackle the range and complexity of ordinary emotional responses to something like *Dallas*?

As might be expected, the insights that do exist into television and everyday emotion were not developed in 'effects' laboratories. A new group of researchers have dropped such methods entirely. Rejecting the idea of forcing their 'experimental subjects' to play with dolls and dummy electric shock generators, they prefer to listen to and analyse what people have to say for themselves about TV. This no doubt looks like heresy to some scientists who, as Cedric Cullingford has commented, will go to amazing lengths to avoid actually talking to children about television. As he says, 'the fact that children can communicate ideas, and can respond to questions is not only overlooked but positively dreaded'. The same, of course, applies to adult subjects, who have only rarely been regarded as capable of commenting intelligently on their viewing.

Probably even more shocking to the white-coated scientists, several of these writers are more interested in the *pleasures* television can offer, than the *damage* it can do. In an article titled *Taking Popular Television Seriously*, Richard Dyer writes that 'What I mean is ... asking why and how programmes are entertaining, why people like them and what children's main experiences of television are. These are serious questions because they take us to the heart of the reason why most people watch television. ...I want to understand what the enjoyment is about. We should ask why certain representations are entertaining. Why is this view of reality enjoyable? Why is that view of what social groups are a pleasure?' Some writers have used their own enjoyment of television as a starting point: Ien Ang's study *Watching Dallas* begins with a statement about her own feelings about the programme, while Richard Dyer's book on Light Entertainment begins with a list of the performers he likes (Cilla Black, Jimmy Tarbuck, Morecombe and Wise) and those he can't stand (Rolf Harris, Cliff Richard, Bob Monkhouse).

In keeping with this approach, when Dorothy Hobson began her research into the much derided soap opera *Crossroads* she set out to find what the fans liked about the programme. Her book is based on lengthy recorded interviews with the programme's fans: she says 'It is only by long and relaxed talks and viewing *with* the audience that any understanding of how people watch television

The life and times of Meg Mortimer, one time boss of the Crossroads motel. Fans followed her decline from being the subject of a special wedding souvenir to telling 'her' confessions to the Daily Star.

can be achieved'.

Some sections of Dorothy Hobson's account of her findings have a slightly surprised tone. Although she was interested in **Crossroads** precisely because of its popularity, she, like Laurie Taylor, was unprepared for the extremes of emotion she uncovered. In particular, the sacking of the serial's long-standing star Noele Gordon triggered reaction ranging from sadness through intense resentment to outright anger. For many viewers – especially the thousands who wrote bitter letters of complaint to Central Television – the departure of Meg Richardson, played by Gordon, was a keenly felt loss. She was, they said, 'a friend' whose company would be missed in much the same way that a real friend would be. Similar emotions plagued the **Brookside** viewer who wrote to the TV Times to 'protest in the strongest terms' at the 'heartless murder of Kate', the character killed during the siege at the Close. These comments do not mean that these viewers thought that Meg Richardson or Kate actually existed: as any reader of novels should know, it is not necessary to believe that a fictional character is real, in order to be moved by their fate.

THE SET IN THE SITTING ROOM

Part of the reason for these intense emotions is the domesticity of the experience of watching television. Kate's violent death happened in the letter writer's own house: the soap opera character had, in effect, been a regular guest in her sitting room. It is this same intimacy which disturbs the clean-up television campaigners – 'Why', they say, 'should I have to have "that" in my home'.

Despite early experiments to transmit programmes into cinemas, television is a decidedly housebound medium. We don't have to leave the home to see it, as we do cinema: it sits in there waiting for us. Although anti-television writers (and the understandably antagonistic cinema industry) depict television as an ominous intruder, research suggests that the majority of viewers regard their sets rather affectionately, seeing them, in Peter Collett's words, as 'part of the family'.

The television manufacturing industry has bolstered this attitude by deliberately downplaying the technological nature of television. Once the early years of uncertain reception and home-built receivers were over, they began selling television as a 'part of the furniture'. By 1950, for instance, **Television Weekly** was able to say 'the accent is on television as part of the home furnishing scheme'. Advertisements suggested that a television should be

chosen to blend with the design of a sitting room, with other units carefully arranged around it. The set itself was transformed into a homely, domestic device with carefully styled cabinets, highly polished veneer finishes, and sometimes, folding doors. Over the years, the sets have undergone a metamorphosis, from hand-crafted walnut cabinets, through Bakelite to the sixties coloured plastic Murphys, presented as an essential element of any fashionable sitting room. But, throughout these changes, the television has stayed a 'domestic' object which, the advertisements argue, should merge with the decor of the room and 'say something' about personal taste.

Paradoxically, this tendency has been further underlined by the current matt-black hi-tech designs. Although these sets no longer look ashamed of their electronic innards, they are still promoted as part of a unified home furnishing 'look'. Ideally, we are told, they should sit alongside a whole series of other similarly cool and industrial objects. But, unlike record, tape and compact disk systems the promotional material for televisions places comparatively little emphasis on technical developments which might give improved reception. Despite the comparatively poor sound from most sets, no manufacturer has really tried to promote sets offering better sound, or additional speakers. TV's, advertisers' research suggests, are chosen either because of reliable brand names, or for the way they look. Customers aren't really interested in thinking about them as technical appliances.

Once the set is purchased or rented, people will tend to use the set in a way that accords with its status as 'friendly object', rather than technical equipment. The Peter Collett tapes suggest that very few people try and watch television in 'ideal' conditions, with the lights dimmed and the set carefully tuned for prime performance. Indeed television engineers can be heard complaining bitterly about the poor quality of reception viewers are prepared to accept.

In some houses, the process of domestication started by the manufacturers will be further exaggerated by the careful placing of objects, photographs and family mementos on top of the set. A flavour of the lengths viewers will go to in adorning their television cabinets is given in a 1947 issue of the magazine **Television Weekly**. In a regular feature called 'Across the Counter, Some Jottings by a Television Dealer' the writer comments that 'a customer once asked "Will it be all right if I put my aquarium on top of my set?"'... Other curious decorations that I have seen poised on top of television cabinets include flora of all species, from miniature palm-trees to cacti; chiming clocks; perspex aeroplanes and pewter pots, an occasional present from Margate; books;

dolls; porcelain animals... and, believe it or not, a fair-sized Christmas tree complete with tinsel, coloured-balls and crackers. It is clear that television sets have other uses besides the obvious ones!'

It has become commonplace to regret the way that television sets have replaced coal fires as the focal points of sitting rooms. Television, it is argued, has blocked family discussions, and stopped people talking to each other. Peter Collett believes, however, that television is more often an aid for conversation than a barrier to it. 'Television is *what* people talk about, while it is on, as well as at work the next day. It buttresses social relationships in the sense that it gives people something to discuss. Often, it provides a kind of focus for people to talk about other things'. David Morley concurs: 'Television is used as a constant supply of common experience between people who don't necessarily know each other very well... At its simplest it is an experience that a lot of people have in common across class barriers, across social divisions of various kinds. The talk may be about television, but very often the point of the conversation is that a relationship is being developed and TV is the easiest form of common experience to refer to as the basis for conversation.'

Television runs through family life as the substance of discussions, arguments and reconciliations, as well as the source of solitary moments of reflection. Janet Brown, member of one of the families filmed by Peter Collett, comments: 'When me and Marie want to have a mother and daughter discussion we will just turn down the television and sit and chat for a couple of hours. I still know what is happening on television, but when I'm having a heart to heart with Marie my sole attention is on her. Actually, a lot of times the programme will actually spark off the discussion. We turn it down so we are watching it *and* having a discussion at the same time.'

This does not mean that all families talk about and over the television. Unhappy families are very different. In these, television viewing can be much closer to images of zombified families, with conversation outlawed, except for quarrels over the choice of programme. Television becomes an excuse for not talking, a way of shutting other people out.

This use of television was graphically demonstrated by the flood of distressing letters written to *Woman* magazine. Many men, it seems, use television to punish their wives. The women's misery is almost palpable. One, who self-deprecatingly describes her letter as the 'meanderings of an average bored housewife', writes 'I HATE TV AND WISH IT HAD NEVER BEEN INVENTED. I really miss having family arguments and discussions. My husband is a lecturer at the local polytechnic so he spends most of his time talking to or at his students. So when he comes down he just wants to relax and watch tv and I am stuck with the company of our three-year-old, longing for real conversation. But night after night on goes that wretched switch. If I complain and he does actually switch *off* then I find I'm too angry to talk! Ironic, but true.' The letters suggest that for many men, television provides an excuse for not facing up to problems in relationships. One letter writer says, 'Regarding its effect on family life, tv just ruins it. That's it in a nutshell. To elaborate, however, it can be a big excuse for not facing up to things'.

Some members of the anti-tv lobby, such as Marie Winn, see television as the direct cause of these domestic traumas. Undoubtedly, it acts as an irritant. But there is little evidence to suggest that these families would be happy ones were it not for the television in the corner: before the days of television newspapers were blamed in exactly the same way. Marital disharmony isn't caused by television any more than playground violence. Television is a device which can be called upon to play many different roles in domestic interaction. For some groups it can act as social glue, binding people together. In others it becomes a potent weapon for wielding against other people, particularly marriage partners.

Depending on the state of your marriage, television is either what you talk about — or an excuse for not talking at all

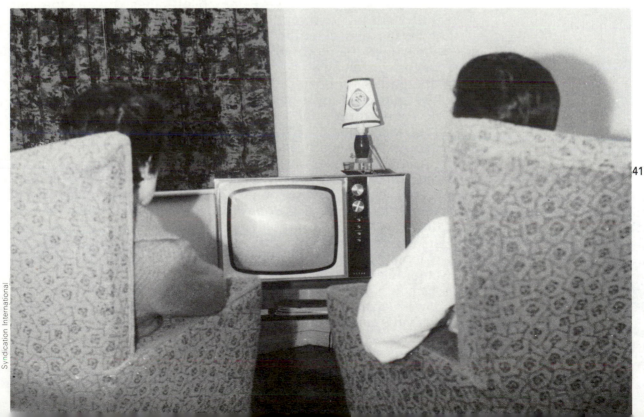

One of the **Woman** correspondents comments perceptively on this. She begins by saying, 'TV made my ex-husband idle, as he would just sit and watch anything. It also helped us to drift apart, as conversation was minimal. If I was to interrupt I was snapped at and told to shut up'. Interestingly, her letter ends in a rather different vein: 'When a family is close in other ways, then tv isn't a threat, it's just another added pleasure and a nice way of resting and putting one's feet up.' Her first marriage finished, she now felt that her experience of television was a complicated reflection of the lack of warmth in the relationship, rather than the direct reason for her unhappiness.

Television can be so vital an element of family interaction that therapists are beginning to use it in discussion sessions. Apparently, conflicts about viewing can be very useful in bringing underlying family tensions to the surface. In particular, male disdain for their wives' choice of programme and ways of viewing can be a graphic signal of the deep-rooted inequalities which still fester inside most marriages. Even the remote control can be a revealing indication of family dynamics. According to David Morley, during peak hours the device can be 'almost like a medieval symbol of power'. In the homes of most of the families he interviewed it sits 'On Daddy's chair and is principally his possession. In some of the Peter Collett tapes you see the man holding the automatic control almost like a mace. It is a very condensed and concrete symbol of authority within the family since it gives the power to change what all the other people in the room are watching'.

The battles for domestic power going on in the living room are often mimicked by similar rows taking place on the screen. Television's forte is the minutiae of human relationships, the ups and downs of domestic life. In particular, it is skilled at offering the frisson of recognition, at reflecting the detail of our everyday lives back at us. Whereas cinema is good at grandeur and epic scale, television characteristically dwells on the small-scale and intimate. This is true even of programmes which claim to be about a majestic sweep of history, such as **Brideshead Revisited** and The **Jewel in the Crown**. Really, when it comes down to it, their stories concern personal relationships and families. The heartland of television is as domesticated as a carefully polished, knick-knack adorned, walnut television cabinet.

Families are everywhere. They populate light entertainment shows such as *Ask The Family*, *The Generation Game*, *Telly Addicts* and *That's Life* and are found in profusion in sit-coms. Just think of the titles: *Steptoe and Son*, *Till Death Us Do Part*, *Not In Front of the Children*, *My Wife Next Door*, *Father Dear Father*, *Relative*

42

Strangers, Man About the House, Home To Roost ... Some of these comic families are genuinely linked by blood ties, others are proxy ones forcibly created by the vicissitudes of flat-sharing, boarding houses or even, as in **Porridge**, prison life. Just like real life, the sit-coms' picture of domesticity isn't always a glowing one. Mostly, the comic moments come from the seedy side of domestic life, the claustrophobia, in-jokes, squabbles and delicate double-crosses.

Domestic life even makes an appearance when the overt substance of a programme is historical or political, since on television almost everything is personalised. The Nazi extermination of the Jews becomes **Holocaust,** and the shifting class relationships in the 1920s become the domestic version of **Upstairs, Downstairs**. The dramatisation of a period through the domestic life of the royal family is a popular variation on this evergreen strategy: The **Six Wives of Henry the Eighth**, **Edward the 7th**, **Edward and Mrs Simpson** are all examples.

The device of looking at the world through the microcosm of family life can also be seen almost every night of the week in factual programmes: in fact, it is almost a rarity to find a documentary which doesn't tell its story through a small group of individuals. In this way, the family, or proxy family, becomes a filter for dealing with everything else. Family sit-com isn't exclusively about family relationships: it is also preoccupied with the ways in which class affects and perverts intimate relationships. Itchy cross-class clashes between people of just slightly different backgrounds have become a comic staple. The **Good Life**, for instance, just wouldn't have been the same without its dissection of what happens when two conflicting middle-class styles meet over the garden fence. Or imagine **Fawlty Towers**, without the excruciating domestic antagonism caused by Basil's upwardly mobile aspirations and his wife's solidly middle-class brashness.

The same detailed look at the foibles of human relationships provides the key to the soap opera. But while sit-coms transform their observations into tightly disciplined comic packages, soap operas show off their knowledge in a more relaxed fashion. The day-to-day detail of family life, source material for sit-coms, takes centre stage: gossip, petty quarrels and misunderstandings, small excitements, those minute details of personal and domestic life are the substance of the British soap operas. Just like their mainly female viewers, the characters spend much of their time juggling the contradictory demands of spouses, friends, parents, children and neighbours, trying to manage money whilst also attempting to carve out satisfactory sexual and emotional partnerships of their own. It can be a hard act to maintain. 'Soap operas', Christine Geraghty says, 'celebrate the undervalued skills of women' in handling intimate relationships.

Serials are not only about these vital mundanities: they also deal with the big events that occasionally erupt into everyday life. But as with the smaller stories, most of these grander plots reflect back the lives of those watching. Landmarks in the soaps' plots correspond to viewers' own turning points: marriages, friendships, deaths, births and divorces.

Of course, as viewers of the affectionate parody *Soap* know, serials, especially American and Australian ones, are marked by an astonishing proliferation of these events. And, they often come extravagantly packaged. Everyone experiences deaths in the family, but how many shoot-outs and brain tumours do most

Upstairs Downstairs **(left) and** Brookside **(right). From costume drama to soap opera, it is impossible to escape the ever present television family.**

people come across? But, stripped down to their bare bones, even the most melodramatic of plots are really 'about' everyday emotions. Kidnappings provide a dramatic way of testing marriages, sieges an investigation of friendships under pressure. Whether it is Southfork Ranch or the Rover's Return, the plots relentlessly return to the same ordinary imponderables: jealousy, romance, illness, the search for a perfect relationship, the best way to bring up a child ...

Soap opera characters live in a complicated world. For them, as for us, nothing will ever be completely resolved or totally worked out. In single plays a wedding can tie everything into a neat 'happy ending'. Soap operas, however, treat marriage as the opportunity

for a whole series of other stories about marital relationships, infidelity and children. Nothing is ever simple. The plots are open-ended and relentlessly criss-crossed, continuing forever into the future. 'Like us, soap opera characters have to live with the consequences', Charlotte Brunsdon says. 'It is usually only when an actor or actress takes the option we haven't got and leaves the programme that there is any chance of a happy ending. Elsie may have gone off to a golden sunset – but what comfort or hope is there for Rita? Or Hilda? Or Mavis, Emily, Bet, or Betty?'

For the committed viewer, part of the enjoyment is the assimilation of the fictional world into everyday life. As the merchandising departments are beginning to realise, there is a

A meeting of some of television's most renowed families: the Queen visits Coronation Street.

Granada Television

special pleasure in letting the ephemera of other communities spill into our sitting rooms. The conversations of the serial become the subjects of real-life conversations, to which star stories from the tabloids add another dimension. Soap operas are tailor-made for gossip because of the accessibility of their worlds. We can see inside all the houses, hear the intimate discussions of all the couples in the Street, know about an errant husband's misdemeanours before he has confessed to anyone. Sooner or later, everyone's personal life is revealed: very little is so private that it is beyond the realm of the camera. As a reward for committed viewing, soap offers us the chance of knowing another world better than we can ever know our own.

These communities run in parallel to ours in more ways than one. Not only do the same kind of things happen as occur in our own lives, but serials maintain the fiction that they live alongside us on the same planet. Recent years have seen a trend for increased geographical specificity: while the *Crossroads* motel used to be amorphously sited 'somewhere outside Birmingham', some residents of Liverpool now really do live in the next street to *Brookside*. In all the soaps, the characters experience the change in seasons when we do, celebrate Christmas and royal events at the same time as us. And life goes on even when we, the viewers, are not there to see it. 'Abandoned at the end of an episode', Christine Geraghty says, the characters will have pursued an 'unrecorded existence' in our absence. When we 'look in' on how things are going on 'The Street', in 'the Square', 'the Close' or at 'the Market' it is with the knowledge that events will have happened since we were last there: conversations will have taken place, storylines inched their way forward.

The real fan has a regular date with 'their' soap opera. Every week, the same time, on the same days, is set aside for a meshing of real and fictional families. Sandra Smith says, 'You can't help but get involved if you watch a programme three or four nights in every week'. For some viewers of *Crossroads* and *Coronation Street*, this pattern will have been going on for the whole of their lives.

For many viewers, the ritual itself increases the enjoyment. Charlotte Brunsdon says, for instance, that part of her reason for watching *Crossroads* is the reassurance offered by its familiarity. Sandra Smith, meanwhile, uses the programme to provide a brief break from housework and childcare. 'That 20 minutes is the longest I sit down all day' she says, 'It's a hectic rush before and a hectic rush afterwards.' For her it is something to look forward to, a special, private part of the day. In the past, a similar pause might have been provided by the delivery of the evening newspaper, a middle-class pre-dinner sherry or even, perhaps, in religious households, family prayers. Soap operas offer the same kind of respite, plus an invigoratingly intimate look into another world.

There are particularly close links between the viewers' lives and soap opera, but the ritual pleasures of watching a familiar series operate for other types of programme, too. The continuous, domestic nature of television has helped to make Saturday afternoon equal television sport for many viewers. For others, Wednesday night belongs to *Minder*, and Saturday evening is *Hill Street Blues*. It is no rarity to find people who outgrew *Dr Who* years ago but still feel Saturday teatime is irrevocably linked to the programme. It is a characteristic of television viewing which has

been noted by the schedulers. Paul Fox, a scheduler for eighteen years says, 'Public expectation is a very, very important thing. Certain days are linked to certain programmes. If you move those programmes from those days they will suffer, there is no question about it. Because public expectations go with these programmes, they won't see the same programme on Tuesday at a different time.'

The role of television in domestic ritual underlines the upset viewers feel when one of their favourites finishes. The end of a series, or the departure of a much loved character leaves a gap and often, it seems, promotes the desire to artificially prolong the relationship. These feelings have helped to make tv tie-in books one of the success stories of 80's publishing, assisted the home

Channel 4

video boom and bolstered the popularity of repeats. Despite critical brickbats about 'too many re-runs', the ratings demonstrate that third and even fourth repeats of popular programmes are well received by audiences, at least some of whom must have already seen them. To give just one example, the highest rated programme over the Christmas week in 1984 was a repeat of **Porridge** seen by 19.4 million viewers, a figure which means it beat the first tv outing of *Raiders of the Lost Ark*.

Long-running programmes can become part of our lives in the way a longstanding, but not particularly well-liked neighbour can be: they might be moaned about, but it is hard to imagine their absence. The enjoyable pull of continuity and ritualised viewing

can become rather paradoxical and self-defeating for the viewer. We can end up hoping that a much-loved programme won't ever change, even when we know deep down that we might actually enjoy it if they did. It is quite possible to know a show has passed its peak and that the dramatic possibilities of a situation have been exhausted, but still bitterly protest at its passing.

Less depressingly, our unwillingness to let go has contributed to the way of writing about fictional characters which pretends that they are free to pursue an independent existence. It was in this spirit that the **Sun** ran stories detailing what happened to the Hunters *after* they were sacked from **Crossroads**. And **Coronation Street's** twenty-five year celebration book gives the current whereabouts of all the major characters in the serial's past. Apparently, Ray Langton now lives in Holland, Lucille Hewitt in Ireland and Marion and Eddie Yeats 'have both settled happily in Bury with a family of their own'. Stranger still, Dot Greenhalgh's entry in the book ends by saying 'her whereabouts are unknown' – as though this would come as a surprise.

Viewers know better. Florrie Lindley (Betty Alberge) isn't in Canada: she recently died from a stroke after living in Brookside Close with her husband, the crotchety Harry Cross. And Elsie Tanner (Pat Phoenix) has exchanged Portuguese beaches for Bridlington where she runs a guest house with **Constant Hot Water**.

The continuous, domestic, nature of television serials and the possibilities for ritualised viewing they offer have helped to make the series and serial into the television form *par excellence*. When the television industry can't, or won't, offer fans these pleasures, the viewers step in and build their own 'serials' by linking the appearances of favoured actors in different programmes. In the fantasies of those watching, the fictional characters slip sideways from one programme to another, just as real-life presenters and entertainers do. The **Radio Times** might have announced *To the Manor Born* as an entirely new situation comedy, but most regular viewers chose to interpret its countrified Sloane heroine as a reincarnation of Margo from **The Good Life**. Laurie Taylor quotes a woman viewer who jokes she always loved Bobby Ewing: even when he had funny eyes and webbed feet in *Man From Atlantis*!

Television itself plays the same kind of games when it brings back old favourites in new forms. **Z-Cars** became **Softly Softly**, and **Danger Man**, **The Prisoner**. And when **The Likely Lads** was revived, the title deliberately mimicked the question everyone was supposed to have been asking: *Whatever Happened to the Likely Lads*? Terry and Bob's bickering friendship is not the only situation comedy to re-appear later in a slightly different form. As the most popular non-serial form of television, the sit-com has become

BBC-1

From Dixon of Dock Green's **'Evening All' to roll call at the** Hill Street Blues **precinct house, police series have provided an enduring Saturday ritual.**

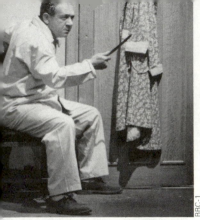

Quasi-families in strife: Sid James and Tony Hancock battle it out.

BBC-1

adept at linking series together as spin-offs, letting, for instance, *Man About the House* beget both *George and Mildred* and *Robin's Nest*. This device also allows script-writers to get round the genre's inbuilt lack of development, which has the sit-com's 'sit' returning back to status quo at the start of each new episode.

As this suggests, serial forms are not only resonant for their viewers. They also have a special importance within the television industry, not least because they are cheap. An on-going serial, or a number of similar series, is far more cost-efficient to make than a set of single plays. With a serial, expensive studios can be booked constantly (and therefore more cost-effectively), sets re-used over and over again, scripts written quickly, actors quickly rehearsed. In contrast to a one-off single play, where only an hour's drama results from comparatively vast expenditure, the serial gives hundreds, possibly thousands, of hours of television for the initial investment.

Several American writers have pointed out that television companies are not so much in the business of producing programmes as 'delivering' audiences to advertisers. In Britain, the BBC is not (yet?) involved in this, but it too needs to gather big ratings in order to justify increases in the licence fee. But the television companies do not simply need to occasionally and unpredictably produce vast audiences. They want to 'maximise' their viewers throughout each evening, *and* as far as possible, be able to guarantee that a certain number of people will be watching.

Soap operas, enjoyed because of their regularity and familiarity, are the vital 'bankers' for the schedulers. 'The drama serials – *Coronation Street*, *Crossroads*, *Emmerdale Farm* – are obviously among the landmarks in the evenings schedule' according to Paul Fox. 'They are the solid audience grabbers. *I know* they are going to get the ratings.' From a basis of soap (and the early-evening news) the schedulers try and 'build' a whole evening's worth of big audiences. 'You come out of *Coronation Street* and into 2 half hours of comedy back to back: that will be very successful', Paul Fox says. 'Then at 9.00 you come into something like *Minder* and *The News at Ten* and you have a very, very good evening'.

Between the 'bankers' are programmes with less certain ratings: the ones that the scheduler must really work hard for. As Michael Pilsworth suggests, 'the art is to build towards the climax, the audience peak, little by little, as the evening progresses. Where low appeal programmes have to be inserted into peak-time schedules, as with the current affairs *World in Action*, *Panorama* and *TV Eye* they are either purposely placed against weak opposition or they are "hammocked"'. This rather strange sounding activity involves placing 'bankers' before and after less popular programmes in the hope that people will keep watching. Paul Fox says 'In between *Crossroads* and *Coronation Street* is undoubtedly a very valuable slot in the schedules. People stay with *Crossroads* until the end, they expect to see *Coronation Street* start in half an hour and so they stay and watch the programme in between. It is a time when there is a certain amount of anticipation and pleasure, a marvellous place to build a show. Yorkshire television was very fortunate in having *Where There's Life* with Miriam Stoppard there. Miriam won the audience over and now *Where There's Life* could go anywhere'.

Just as there is now pressure on television companies to produce serials rather than single plays, so the needs of the

BBC-1

schedule mean other constraints. If a new programme is to be neatly hammocked between *Crossroads* and *Coronation Street* it cannot be anything other than a perfect 26 minutes long: the 'ITV half-hour' which, with advertisments, fills the gap between the programmes. Films of 'difficult' lengths and long 'specials' which need to be divided to fit around the 9.00 or 10.00 news create problems for the schedule and are penalised by this system. Increasingly, some writers have argued, the tendency is to contract or expand planned programmes into an hour or half-hour slot, regardless of whether that is actually the best length for the subject.

In opposition to these ideas, it has also been suggested that time slots which are unwieldy for the schedule also present problems for viewers. Paul Fox, for instance, argues that 'phoney times like 7.40 and 8.10 are anti-audience'. 'People' he says, 'like a regular time: they want programmes starting on the hour and half hour. One of the old fashioned things about the BBC is that they are stuck with these kinds of times because their so-called hour long programmes are actually 52 minutes for showing in America with commercials. When I was at the BBC I moved *The News* from 9.10 to 9.00. It was one of the achievements I was really proud of. It was a major thing to do.

Some people would be appalled by the suggestion that a ten minute alteration in the schedules might really affect people. For them, it would be further evidence of the scheduler's Svengali-like power to manipulate audiences, by forcing us to watch programmes we would otherwise avoid and, possibly even more sinister, structuring our days for us. And, it is true that television almost invisibly reminds us what we should be doing when. The days of the 'toddler's truce', with all programmes banned between six and seven so mothers could put children to bed are now over, but television still tries to tell us when it is time to eat tea, when we can relax, and perhaps most strictly, what time to go to bed. We are, it seems, faced with a new version of the old cyclic problem about the 'effects' of television. Are our evenings the way they are because of the television schedules? Or are the schedules structured the way they are because of our evenings?

For the most part, the schedulers themselves do not believe their power is absolute. They know that while careful positioning may persuade us to 'taste' a programme, it is unlikely to make us stay with it if we are unimpressed. In the same way, many schedulers prefer to see their work as a fallible skill involving delicate predictions about people's lives and desires, than an absolute science. For instance, Paul Fox comments, 'I believe scheduling is an art in that it combines judgement, intuition, gut feeling, knowledge, experience, all of those things.' It is, in Michael Pilsworth's words, 'a tricky skill' and 'an imperfect art'. How can it be otherwise, Pilsworth says, 'when 11 million people stay up late to watch a darts programme; when sheep dog trials and snooker produce surprisingly large audiences; or when glossy American series flop (observe the fate of *Time Express* or *Mrs Columbo*) or become a national cult (*Dallas*)'. In fact, although scheduling seems likely to become an increasingly vital aspect of the television industry, the results of simple scheduling 'tricks' like hammocking may decline as people become used to switching channels and more adept with remote controls and videos.

As well as intuition about what is likely to be a hit and what the

opposing channels are planning, the effective scheduler needs a keen sense of how social life and patterns of viewing are shifting. They must be able to evaluate the ways people fit television in with their other activities: for, as we have seen, the texture of people's lives is far too complicated for programmes simply to be imposed. It was probably a miscalculation in this last, crucial, area that contributed to the failure of the new soap operas The *Practice* and *Albion Market* to become ratings failures. Friday and Sunday nights, when they were shown, are too dissimilar in mood and activities to offer the ritualised pleasures usually associated with soap opera. In addition, these evenings are usually considered the preserve of family viewing. Women, always the most important group of viewers for any new soap, may not have been able to make a firm claim for 'their' programmes on these nights. Out of sync with the lives of the majority of their potential viewers, The *Practice* and *Albion Market* became widely seen as victims of poor scheduling.

Viewers' relationships with the schedule are much like their relationships with the rest of television. On the one hand, the people who own, manage and produce television have the ability to make a decision which greatly affects their lives. Schedules are a framework around which we must fit. But at the same time as

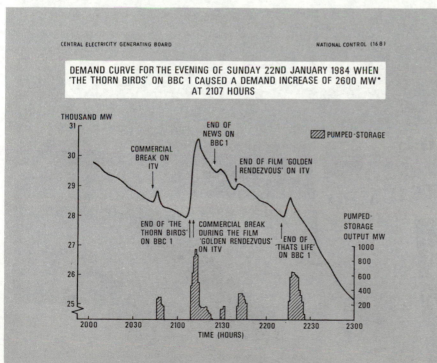

CENTRAL ELECTRICITY GENERATING BOARD   NATIONAL CONTROL (16 8)

DEMAND CURVE FOR THE EVENING OF SUNDAY 22ND JANUARY 1984 WHEN 'THE THORN BIRDS' ON BBC 1 CAUSED A DEMAND INCREASE OF 2600 MW* AT 2107 HOURS

The Central Electricity Generating Board provides another way of measuring audiences. Here, their graph shows the massive demand for electricity at the end of The Thorn Birds. **Millions of viewers turned on lights, made tea and used electrically-pumped water to flush their toilets.**

53

television has the power to affect our lives, we also have the ability to use it for our own ends. We do not have to passively accept the hints and nudges it offers: as active viewers we can, and will, reject programme times when they clash with our own existing habits and desires. Rather than being endlessly structured and manipulated by television, we creatively fit it into our lives.

Television's never-ending fascination with the monarchy means that royal rituals have become broadcasting rituals.

TELEVISION PREJUDICES   3

The architect Frank Lloyd Wright once said that television was 'chewing gum for the eyes'. It is an evocative phrase, conjuring up a particularly unpleasant image of the zombified television viewer, endlessly, unthinkingly, masticating. But this insignificant sugary commodity has more qualities than simple chewy blandness: it has a nationality. Wherever it is actually manufactured, chewing gum is a symbol of Americana. To those who despise it, it is an incarnation of every unnecessary, disposable and dangerous aspect of the American way of life.

Many people have similarly powerful responses to American television programmes, seeing them as soporific, mind-numbing drivel. As Geoffrey Lealand notes in his study *American Television Programmes on British Screens* 'one often waits for the following epithets to follow any mention of an American television programme: ''mindless'', ''glossy'', ''shallow'', ''junk'', ''inane'', ''pap'', ''bilge'', ''bland, brainless and boring''... The climate of general disapproval is such that it is a brave critic who goes into print defending an American programme'. One such writer is *Times* critic Elkan Allan: note, however, the apologetic cast to an end-of-year round-up. 'For me, five of the most enjoyable programmes of the year were despised American series. It may not be fashionable to say so, but I found *Rhoda*, *Dallas*, *Knot's Landing* the repeats of *The Rockford Files*, and above all, *Hill Street Blues* far superior to any British equivalents'.

Elkan Allan may be embarrassed to admit his fondness for *Dallas* but the programme's position in the ratings suggests an interesting gap between the tastes of Allan's peer group, and those of the majority of viewers. Amongst the latter, passion is more common than reticence. Many found the period when the series was off the screen after being poached by Thames so frustrating that they hired them on cassette. It was reported that fans on the South coast were tuning into the French channel TF1 to watch the missing episodes dubbed into French.

The BBC may have been anxious to retrieve *Dallas*, but this did not stop Alasdair Milne, Director General of the BBC from coining the phrase 'wall to wall *Dallas*' to refer to television at its very worst. Milne's phrase

DA
FEV

BANK
night. At
nasty ol'
Streets and

SUSPECT 1
Lusty Dusty . . . Sue Ellen's
rugged cowboy lover

Victim J.R. . . . even he doesn't kr

SUSPECT 2
Sexy Sue Ellen . . . J.R.'s
long-suffering young wife

PICTURE SPECIAL ON TH

implies that the Southfork saga is not so much a highly popular American-style soap opera as an unending strip of mass produced carpet; bland, identical throughout the roll and purchased by the yard.

Some of this dislike is fuelled by genuine fears of cultural imperialism: fears that the multi-million dollar American entertainment industries will overwhelm indigenous cultures. Understandably, many people are disturbed by the prospect of children growing up more familiar with events at Southfork Ranch than in their own countries. When the children in question live in circumstances where *Dallas* lifestyles are unimaginable, these fears are reinforced. Such conspicuous consumption of luxuries, many critics have argued, is nothing more than an empty

The Sun

Dallas: the televisual equivalent of wall to wall carpeting?

promise of 'jam tomorrow': window-dressing for ruthless American capitalism.

At the same time, members of the television industry in Britian and elsewhere are worried that American imports may result in fewer home-based productions, causing unemployment and damaging the domestic television industry. This possibility is increased by the relatively low export sale prices accepted by some American companies. American programmes designed for sale throughout the world can cover their production costs on their huge home market. All foreign sales are pure profit. Consequently, producers can afford to undercut competing programmes from countries with smaller audiences and production set-ups. Before the 'poaching' row, the BBC was apparently only paying £29,000 per episode of *Dallas* — a figure which would barely pay for the cheapest and shortest home-produced programme.

Despite the doom-laden prophecies of writers like Herbert Schiller and Jeremy Tunstall, the title of whose book *The Media Are American* epitomises this perspective, few countries are entirely prostrate at the feet of the American production companies. Certainly in the case of Britain, fears about being swamped by American programmes should be seen in the context of Britain's own success in the international television market, which is second only to that of America. Neither are American productions automatically successful around the world: *Dallas* was a miserable failure in Japan, just as the number one American programme *The Cosby Show* has been here so far.

Although American programmes are not always roaring successes when exported, it is undeniable that the basic programme types first developed by American TV have swept the world: versions of the police series, for example, can be found almost everywhere. There are even national versions of *Dallas* such as *Chateauvallon* in France and *Herrenstraat 10* in the Netherlands, created partly as responses to fears of American cultural imperialism. Some writers have suggested, however, that they are simply further symptoms of the same problem and argue that having a French or Dutch JR does not necessarily make the series any more relevant.

In Britain, these accusations have been particularly levelled at 'mid-Atlantic' programmes produced with at least half an eye on foreign sales. Increasingly, it has become hard for any mid-to-high budget programme to get made without co-production money from a foreign source. This, many critics would claim, encourages an unchallenging conformity. The tell-tale signs, they say, are unsuitable, but bankable, international 'names' recruited to play leading roles (sometimes as a package of one star 'name' from each of the funding countries) and an over-emphasis on the touristy aspects of a country's past. In fact, prestigious 'quality' productions like *Tender is the Night* or *Brideshead Revisited* are just as much products of the international market for television programmes

as *Dallas*. Without their co-production money neither would probably have been made. But, these types of programmes are not usually uppermost in the minds of critics examining the American influence on British television. Instead, they tend to dwell on programmes which they see as having an American *look* and *feel*, without necessarily being made in America. The phrase 'wall to wall *Dallas*' is also used to refer to programmes such as *Dempsey and Makepeace* (a British programme with a pronounced American style), *The Price is Right* (a British programme derived from an American format) and *Sons and Daughters* (an Australian afternoon soap opera). 'Wall to wall *Dallas*' has become a codeword for programmes that are 'popular', 'glossy', 'internationally understandable' and 'clearly commercial', rather than simply 'American'.

Often, the phrase suggests a distaste for generic serials and series as a whole, from soap operas to cop shows. As we saw in the last chapter, part of the pleasure of these programmes is the way each new episode is partly the same as, and partly different, from the last. 'Wall to wall *Dallas*' leaves out the vital element of 'difference'. It suggests, instead, that every episode of an American style series is identically mind-numbing and soporific — and that the series and serials themselves are all equally bland and interchangeable.

The idea that English 'high culture' is in danger of being swamped by a relentless deluge of Americana is not new. Author Dick Hebdige traces these fears back to at least the nineteen-thirties, when writers as different as the conservative Evelyn Waugh and the socialist George Orwell were united by a fascinated loathing for modern architecture, holiday camps, advertising, fast food, plastics, and of course, chewing gum. To both Waugh and Orwell, these were the images of a soft, enervating, easy life which threatened to smother British cultural identity, dragging the whole culture down into an amoral morass.

During the war, these patrician fears were enhanced by resentment at the visiting GIs' consumer goods and 'excessive' sexuality. By the fifties, the lines were drawn: real working-class culture, quality and taste on one side; the ersatz blandishments of 'soft', 'disposable' commodities, streamlined cars, rock and roll, crime, promiscuity on the other. Dick Hebdige says 'Whenever anything "American" was sighted, it tended to be read, at least by those working in the context of education or professional cultural criticism, as the begining of the end... the very mention of America could summon up a cluster of other associations. It could be used to contaminate others words and concepts by sheer proximity as in "Americanised sex", "the false values of the American film" etc'.

Hebdige describes how 'images of crime, disaffected youth, urban crisis and spiritual drift are anchored together around "popular" American commodities... fixing a chain of associations ...which has since become thoroughly sedimented in British common sense'. In particular,

American food became a standard metaphor for declining standards. The middle-aged narrator of Orwell's **Coming Up For Air** experiences the depths of despair with a synthetic sausage. Countless writers use McDonald's hamburgers as a shorthand image for the 'falsity' of modern life. Very few seem to fear an increase in the number of Italian, Chinese and French restaurants in quite the same way.

Since the derogatory link between television viewing and the passive consumption of food is already well established (see Chapter One), the comparison between American food and television has an especially revolting resonance. Contemporary anti-imperialist critiques of American programmes employ almost exactly the same metaphors as Orwell used fifty years ago. Martin Esslin, for instance, writes 'As American breakfast cereals, American soft drinks, American pop music and American industrial practises spread in Europe, the American folk heroes also, inevitably, take over the fantasy world of the Europeans.'

At the beginning of the fifties fears about a 'diet of Americana' were concentrated on the campaign to save the BBC's monopoly on broadcasting. To many, the introduction of commercial television, which was supported by a coalition of interests in the entertainment industries and the business lobby of the Conservative party, looked like the start of a dangerous slide towards chaos. Christopher Mayhew, a vociferous anti-commercial television campaigner, claimed in his pamphlet **Dear Viewer** that the 'Americanisation' of television, especially the introduction of advertising, would lead to 'unending banality'. He asked his readers to 'exercise all the influence you have, as a citizen of the most democratic country in the world, to prevent this barbarous idea being realised'. In the House of Commons debate on the Television Bill Americanisation was uppermost in many speaker's minds: Lord Esher regretfully said that the British showed 'an orderly and admirable quiet as we sit among the ruins of our wealth listening to the ugly noises set up by the rest of the world.' Commercial television, he said, would be 'a planned and premeditated orgy of vulgarity'. The Bill became law in 1954 — with a clause stipulating that 'a proper proportion of recorded and other matter had to be of British origin and performance'. That limitation is still enshrined in British broadcasting. Currently, the percentage of non-British/non-EEC programmes allowed on independent television by the IBA is 14%. In theory, this same figure is kept to by the BBC.

Fears about 'American-style commercialisation' resurfaced in 1961 with the Pilkington Committee's report on the future of broadcasting. The majority of the committee's members decided that ITV had failed to uphold 'standards'. They argued loudly, but in vain, (the report was shelved) that the whole future of independent television should be reconsidered. A metaphor of sticky senselessness suggested by candyfloss, a synthetic American-style food, provides the tone of the report. It also runs throughout the influential book **The Uses of Literacy** written by Professor Richard Hoggart, the man widely believed to be the main voice behind the Pilkington committee. In part, Hoggart's book is a detailed appreciation of old-fashioned working-class community life (*Coronation Street* is almost a dramatisation of its first few chapters). In later pages, however, the book becomes a critique of the homogenising impact of American life. According to **The Uses of Literacy** 'authentic' working-class life is being destroyed by the 'hollow brightness', 'shiny barbarism' and 'spiritual decay' of imported American culture. The phrases could have come from almost any of Waugh or Orwell's novels.

The political and industrial reality behind both Hoggart's book and the Pilkington Report was the immense popularity of ITV. At the beginning of commercial television the BBC had been arrogantly convinced

Lucille Ball and Desi Arnez in I Love Lucy: **the American import which featured on the cover of the first** Television Times.

that audiences would prefer its own rather sedate and sometimes condescending brand of television, to 'Americanised rubbish'. Although theoretically committed to uplifting the whole nation, the reality of the BBC's concept of public service broadcasting was somewhat different. In 1954 it amounted to giving a particular, middle class audience educational programmes, direct transmissions of light West End theatrical hits, parlour games and classical music. Other 'publics' were not served at all. There was hardly any original drama and no series or serials. When, on the eve of ITV, a belated attempt was made to catch up with **Dixon of Dock Green** and the first soap opera **The Grove Family**, the opposition from within the BBC Drama Department was so great that these programmes had to be produced by Light Entertainment instead. That department was something of a poor relation: as Peter Black notes in **The Mirror in the Corner**, his book about the start of ITV, it's head had to fight 'the mysterious, unattributable body of BBC opinion which recognised that light entertainment had to exist, but regretted the necessity, and was just as likely to feel shame at its successes as pride'.

The BBC's certainty about its unassailable place in British life was such that it experienced a major body blow when the majority of its audience departed. By September 1957, ITV had gained (stolen, in the BBC's eyes) 79% of the audience, as 'easily as a picnicking family will strip a hedge of blackberries', according to Peter Black. As he says 'the audience's goodwill towards the monopoly turned out to be an illusion. Once they had a choice, the working-class left the BBC at a pace that suggested ill will was more deeply entrenched than good.'

Regardless of the BBC's predictions, a good percentage of the audience actually enjoyed the advertisements on commercial television and preferred American-style popular programmes such as **Take Your Pick**, **People are Funny**, **Emergency – Ward 10** and imports like **Dragnet** and **I Love Lucy**. They liked the less patronising presentation of the new channel, and responded well to the entertainment-oriented philosophy which quickly took centre stage after some initial dabbling in BBC-ish public service. Roland Gillette, from Associated Rediffusion, probably the brashest of the new companies, crudely, but accurately described the situation: 'Lets face it once and for all. The public likes girls, wrestling, bright musicals, quiz shows and real life drama. We gave them the Halle orchestra, Foreign Press Club, floodlit football and visits to the local fire station. Well, we've learned. From now on, what the public wants, it's going to get.' Other independent companies like Granada were more restrained, but something of the same ethos was soon apparent throughout ITV.

The BBC was forced into a dramatic re-think. Some of the excesses of the educational face of public service were abandoned, along with the uncompromising schedules and the stark, faceless presentation of

The News. Popular programmes like *Grandstand* and *The Black and White Ministrel Show* were introduced and the hour between 6.00 and 7.00 was filled with the sharp and irreverent *Tonight*. The BBC even tried a youth programme, *Six-Five Special*, judged a success by *Photoplay* magazine for being 'so strictly un-BBC'. By the early sixties, the Corporation, under the Director-Generalship of Hugh Carleton Greene, was leading the way in several popular genres, especially popular drama (*Z-Cars*), situation comedy (*Steptoe and Son*) and, in a slightly more highbrow fashion, satire (*That Was the Week That Was*, a spin-off from *Tonight*).

Sidney Newman's move from ITV to the BBC in 1963 was a vital symbol of this revitalisation. With the ABC company's *Armchair Theatre*

Slick, sexy and occasionally perverse, The Avengers **combined American style gloss with British settings and British stars.**

The Sunday Despatch **celebrates the start of commercial television — professionals preferred the more sanitised sound of 'independent' television.**

What you are going to see at the start of —

The screen lights up on THURSDAY for the great new entertainment

Sunday Dispatch, SEPTEMBER 18, 1955

COMMERCIAL TELEVISION

Bob Hope   Joy Shelton   Norman Wisdom   Lucille Ball

THE television set in your living-room will on Thursday start to provide vastly more, brighter, and better entertainment than it ever has before. That evening the London programme contractors for commercial television, Associated-Rediffusion Ltd., and Associated Broadcasting Company, combine forces to present a gala opening. Subsequently A-R will give Monday-Friday show. ABC week-end programmes

see the latest gadgets in the home, and shop with Elizabeth Allan.

American picture shorts will bring Roy Rogers, Hopalong Cassidy and Mickey Rooney to the screen, and Lucille Ball in "I Love Lucy."

Weekday programmes

Associated-Rediffusion, Ltd.

10.45 a.m. to 12.30 p.m.—Morning Magazine, a miscellany of news, interviews, serials, and talks abo fashion.

★ The new television programmes will open up for viewers the biggest give-away the country has ever known. Studio audiences may get anything from a stick of toffee rock to

Newman had developed a reputation for producing aggressive, innovatory television drama aimed at and about 'the people who own TV sets — which is the working class'. Under his guidance, *The Wednesday Play* produced direct and shocking plays like *Up The Junction* and *Cathy Come Home*.

Appreciations of *The Wednesday Play* often ignore the fact that Newman was Canadian rather than British, and that his talents with drama were used in America, at NBC, before he was 'discovered' by the British. Although the Pilkington Committee chose to deny it, there was more to the American influence on British television than simply an influx of quiz shows and the introduction of commercial breaks. Such evidence, however, sits very uneasily with the images of Americana inherited from Waugh, Orwell and Hoggart.

The introduction of commercial television coincided with the period when a new, youth-oriented working-class leisure culture was developing. Americana played a central part in this energetic rejection of national heritage. Teenagers were attracted to the dynamism and exuberance of American fashions, music, films and products such as streamlined cars, extravagant male fashions, transistor radios, 'modern' styling, plastics. 'Things English' by contrast, looked fusty, conventional and conservative.

Only some of these elements found their way into British-produced television programmes, partly because youth culture sat uneasily in a medium obsessed with family units and domesticity. But, something of the same basic dynamism which the teenagers of the fifties admired in American music is also widely appreciated in American televison. The people interviewed for Geoffrey Lealand's research enjoyed the overall *feel* of American programmes, especially the action, excitement and faster-moving pace of programmes like *Dallas* and *Hill Street Blues*. Every single episode of *Dallas* contains a vast number of events, mostly of an intense and dramatic nature. British television, by comparison, has always been more at home with the slower, more naturalistic speed of ordinary lives.

British soap operas are good at dealing with real-life emotions and the detail of domestic life: *Dallas* and *Dynasty* offer the same feelings spiced with larger than life fantasy and languid images of sexual passion. The accusation that the characters in *Dallas* and *Dynasty* display their consumer goods and sexual desires too ostentatiously is almost identical to war-time complaints about the visiting GIs. In fact the old catch-phrase 'over-sexed, over-paid and over here' almost perfectly sums up many people's attitudes to JR and Alexis.

To many schooled in the British tradition of token nods towards grimy realism, there is something positively indecent about the way American television revels in up-front stylisation and surface gloss. But, many of the 1,200 viewers covered by Lealand's survey commented very

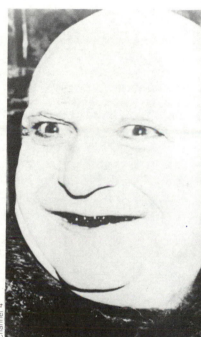

Channel 4

Uncle Fester from The Adams Family. **Far from being emphemeral and easily forgotten American pap, the series was remembered fondly enough by viewers for** Channel Four **to repeat it nearly twenty years later.**

positively on the sensuous 'look' produced by the elegant clothes and glamorous locations of American series.

Miami Vice, described by *The Listener* as 'a slick, youth-oriented blend of cops, cocaine and promos' is a case in point. The slickest of the recent batch of imports, its huge success (especially with a young, working class and black audience) was almost entirely due to its original combination of the action elements of the police series with the look, sound (and limited narrative content) of a music video. The grandiose tracking slots and vivid set-pieces involving neon lights, watery reflections and designer clothes stand as ample evidence for that other quality American programmes are able to offer the viewer: money. Designed to be sold throughout the world, top-notch American productions like *Miami Vice* and *Dynasty* boast a level of funding which would be unimaginable in a British programme aimed solely at the British market. The only other places on television where comparable production values can be seen are in commercials and pop promos. Unsurprisingly, viewer appreciation and critical distaste for these forms run almost equally high.

Production values aren't everything, however. Gameshows are distinguished by their cheapness: in fact, one producer has claimed that 'only a man reading from a lectern costs less'. This did not bother audiences who were impressed, amongst other things, by the apparent value of the prizes. In fact, according to Peter Black 'if any single programme innovation can be said to have won the mass audience (away from the BBC) it was the giveaway shows.' It is interesting, however, that genuine fears about what the cheapness of gameshows means for the overall economy of television have often been obsured by a nervous distaste for the people who take part in, and enjoy, these programmes. Some journalists have nothing but contempt for the people who 'exhibit' themselves on game shows: the music paper *Sounds*, calls *The Price is Right* contestants 'the stupid bastard general public'. 'They leap up and down shout at the audience and generally goofball their way along. They come on really hammy like they are doing a whole lot more than guessing the price of a travelling alarm clock'.

More benevolent condescension permeates an article in *Stills* magazine by Stephen Dark. He says, 'one motivation for watching *The Price is Right* is to see ordinary people unable to cope with the mechanics of stardom... Amid the tacky settings and the humiliating games of chance, no information is given about the participants as they are pushed through a fragmented, conveyor-belt process that reduces them to the level of the disposable consumer products they are offered'. According to these visions, game shows transform people into stupid dupes and automatons, an image worryingly reminiscent of the attitudes to 'the mass' discussed in Chapter One.

Laurie Taylor, however, suggests that rather than being duped, contestants and viewers 'willingly and consciously submit to the engineered thrills of show-biz'. 'You don't look at the big dipper at a fairground and say ''My word this is contrived and calculated, there must be some cynical people behind this, deciding to put the water jump here and the slide there''. Not a bit of it. You say this is a fairground, you pay your money, have a ride, get off gasping at the end and then go off with your arms around each other. People aren't duped by *The Price is Right*, they bring their culture with them to it, just like people going to look at the Blackpool lights'.

Part of the problem stems from the way both the left and right are obsessed by the working classes in their productive capacity: in the factory, in the office, in the docks. In particular, left of centre critics, from Orwell to Hoggart, have great difficulty in dealing with the ways in which working class people actually spend their free time. A great socialist romance has sprung up with traditional pastimes: folk singing, live football and works outings. By contrast, the new working-class forms of leisure which grew up in the nineteen-fifties are looked on with distaste.

Although the audience for game shows is partly composed of solid Labour Party voters, the left tends to view such programmes with a nervous horror reminiscent of Evelyn Waugh. A middle-class dislike of cheap glamour and unrestrained, noisy behaviour becomes confused with a genuine critique of the connection game shows make between happiness and possession of consumer items. Depression at the hostesses' absurd role as display mannequins and the sexist jokes about mother-in-laws becomes merged with a suburban distaste for the gleeful vulgarity of many popular working-class entertainments. Although dressed up as a political argument, many of the left's criticisms of game shows are dependent on quite reactionary definitions of 'good taste'. Would attitudes to *The Price is Right* be different if it offered prizes the writers would want in their own sitting rooms?

Equivalent confusion surrounds the question of the consumerism of game shows. Do the prizes have a corrupting effect, encouraging contestants to humiliate themselves for the chance of a prize while viewers wallow in passive envy? Are they responsible for placing 'the spectator/participant, as representative of that great subordinate class, the public, in a position of direct subordination beneath the icons of capitalism' as one academic writer has charged.

Certainly, all game shows are structured around the question of who will win the prizes: without them, they wouldn't make sense. Alan Boyd, Head of Light Entertainment at London Weekend Television says 'some shows need desire — I used to say greed but the Americans told me they are 'desire shows'. *Play Your Cards Right* is specifically designed to have a prize. We couldn't do it without prizes'. It is less certain what role the prizes play for viewers and potential contestants. The chance to win things is undoubtedly an inducement, but few entrants seem

65

motivated purely by acquisitiveness: indeed, one of the ironies of game shows is that the selection procedures weed out anyone in real need.

Game show participants and viewers are not simply fools duped by the blandishments of commercial television. It is dangerous (and in the case of the media imperialism thesis about the third world, bordering on the racist) to imagine that people only like American programmes because they are manipulated dupes who have somehow been fooled by cheap glamour.

Richard Dyer suggests that musicals and light entertainment shows offer a utopian vision of a world full of direct, unambiguous energy and human potential. For him, the appeal of entertainment shows is partly their magical sense of 'abundance', a feeling he defines as 'the con-

Respectable and unrepectable quiz shows: the antique programme Going For A Song **and Bob Monkhouse on** Bob's Full House.

quest of scarcity, having enough to spare without a sense of the poverty of others, enjoyment of sensuous material reality'. Certainly, the ritual of the conveyor belt loaded with gifts at the end of *The Generation Game* and the final Showcase Showdown in **The Price is Right** is as much a celebration of an exuberant array of prizes as a straightforward appreciation of their economic value. The big thrill of watching (or playing) is that the winner might get the decanter and the clock and the teasmade and the canteen of cutlery and the folding chairs and the holiday. It is the display of abundance which is the point of watching, rather than a simple materialistic calculation of the monetary value of the objects: even though this is ostensibly the central focus of **The Price is Right**.

SOAP STORIES

Alasdair Milne's metaphor of wall to wall carpeting has something of a prep school 'cold baths and discipline' feel about it. The trouble with *Dallas*, Milne's remark implies, is that it is too comfortable, too soft. Similiar fears lurk behind many of the images George Orwell and Richard Hoggart use in their assaults on 'Americanised' popular culture. They worry about 'warm-water baths', 'sunbathing' and the easy life. 'Candy-floss', Hoggart's favourite metaphor, carries connotations of effeminacy: the substance has the sweetness of sugar and the look and texture of a 'powder-puff'. The muscle and masculinity of the British industrial working class, they suggest, is under attack from an excess of Americana, characterised by passivity, leisure and domesticity.

Television, as we saw in the last chapter, plugs directly into these same fears. The activity of viewing takes place in the home, in a 'woman's world' away from the 'male' realms of work and action. For Arthur Seaton, the virile young rebel of *Saturday Night and Sunday Morning*, the sight of his father slumped listlessly in front of the television set epitomises everything which he must rebel against. Arthur, played by Albert Finney, leaves the house in disgust, determined his manhood will never be similarly threatened. In *A Kind of Loving*, another sixties kitchen-sink film, television separates the hero from his father. Trapped into domesticity by a casual girlfriend's pregnancy, he is forced to watch television with her and her mother, thereby missing the 'authentic', male ritual of going out to hear his father's brass band.

These films represent a particularly extreme view of the place of television, identifying the device itself with passivity and femininity. Such fears are usually clustered around certain forms of television, like soap opera, which have come to be seen as especially associated with women. Although more men watch soap operas then might be expected, programmes like *Crossroads* and *Emmerdale Farm* are marketed primarily at a female audience, and are usually thought of as 'women's television'. As we saw in the last chapter, the more traditional soap operas, such as *Crossroads*, portray a women's world, dealing almost exclusively with women's problems and women's stories. Most of the stories are about domestic life, families and unrequited female passion for unattainable (or impossibly flawed) men. In line with this, most of the male characters are either sad or bad: sorry problem-boys ripe for nurturing or shallow, glamorous, matinee idol types. Compare, for instance, the rather fey charm of long running heart throbs David Hunter and Adam Chance of *Crossroads* with the toughness and comparative complexity of the series' matriarchs Meg Mortimer and Nicola Freeman.

The femininity of soap operas is further underlined by the adver-

Indian landscapes and romantic passion in the 'soapy' popular hit. The Far Pavilions **and the quality series** The Jewel in the Crown.

tisements for domestic products, cheapish cosmetics and toiletries which tend to fill the intervals in, and between, programmes. Advertisers assume that while men may be present in the room when the television is on, it is women who will be watching most intently: for them, there is no doubt about the 'gender of the genre'. In fact, the description 'soap opera' has become so closely identified with a female audience that programmes aimed at and about women often tend to be wrongly labelled as soaps. For instance, the female prisoner-of-war series *Tenko*, described as a soap by *The Sunday Times*, could have been far more accurately thought of as period drama.

The fact that soap operas are seen as female has helped to bring the whole form into disrepute. Just like needlework, which was demoted from an art to a craft when it started to be seen as a female rather than a male skill, soap opera suffers from the status of its viewers. It is like women's talk: conventionally refered to as 'chat' or 'gossip', rather than 'conversation'.

While cultural critics may actively dislike popular genres aimed at men, like action adventure series, these programmes are rarely the target of such derision as soap opera. In fact, the word 'soap' is sometimes used as a catch-all phrase for the worst of all television. Almost any programme which fails to achieve the heights it aimed at can be attacked with the term 'soap' — from the sloppily produced drama series described as 'soapy', to the news broadcasts *The Guardian* feared were 'turning into a branch of soap opera'.

Traditionally, the BBC has been extremely wary of soap, despite productions such as *The Grove Family*, *Compact* and *The Newcomers*. In 1982, for instance, *Titbits* magazine had announced 'Soap operas won't wash with the Beeb' and quoted a BBC spokesman as saying 'Soap opera is a term we would never use about any of our programmes... We think there are more interesting ways of putting drama on the screen'. Granada television are similiarly concerned: their insistence that *Coronation Street* is not a soap opera is so strong they refuse to allow extracts from the programme to be shown in the context of the other soaps.

It was therefore interesting to find that one of the most obvious uses of the term 'soap' as an insult involved the BBC. In January 1984 the company was the centre of a storm of criticism over the *Thorn Birds*, a series which Jean Smith of *The Scotman* described as 'The present day equivalent of what used to be dismissively called ''a women's picture''.' An American melodrama from a best-selling Australian romantic book, the series dealt, in classic soap fashion, with the forbidden sexual desires of two women, one much older than the hero. True to form, the hero was, in Jean Smith's words 'a bit of a wimp' and was played by Richard Chamberlain, best known for his performance as soap star Dr. Kildare.

Granada Television

Foolishly, in retrospect, the BBC chose to promote *The Thorn Birds* as their alternative to Granada's lush production of *The Jewel in the Crown*. It was a move they were to regret: *The Thorn Birds'* stress on emotion, and its glossy American look helped make it a stick for various antagonistic parties to beat the BBC with. *Spectator* critic Richard Ingrams said that the BBC had 'betrayed its ancient calling'; Douglas Hurd, Home Office Minister with responsibility for broadcasting, leaked an unattributed statement to the effect that 'the BBC's purchase of the melodrama *The Thorn Birds* has substantially weakened its case for an increase in the television license fee'. The statement, in effect a governmental definition of 'bad' television, went on to say 'the BBC seems to have given up to ITV the role of maintaining broadcasting standards'.

This use of the term 'soap' often suggests something syrupy and excessively emotional. Like the cinematic melodramas and 'women's pictures' which preceeded them, soap operas at their purest deal with feelings rather than action. Critics often describe soap operas as soppy, inconsequential and effeminate. They are not the only people who take this attitude, however: in her research on *Crossroads* viewers, Dorothy Hobson found that many women were ridiculed by their husbands for watching such sloppy stuff. David Morley's interviews with viewers found similar evidence: the majority of men found it hard to admit they they liked fiction at all, as though to admit this would somehow reflect badly on their masculinity. Many would only tolerate fiction when it was seen as 'realistic'.

At times it seems as if the portrayal of emotion — the heart of soap opera — is the problem. But, soap operas are not the only emotive programmes on television. Extravagant displays of feeling by men also provide the heart of 'quality' dramas like *Boys From the Blackstuff* and *Brideshead Revisted*. And in a very different way, the relationship between fellow *Hill Street Blues* policemen Renko and Bobby Hill is passionate in the extreme, the ebb and flow as tempestuous and heart-wrenching as anything between Sue Ellen and JR. The tone and setting for this emotion is different, however, with feelings revealed in the context of work, rather than a domestic situation. Although the people who work in the precinct stationhouse are in many ways like an idealised family, intimacy comes through shared tasks and experiences, often in the face of violence and danger, rather than from purely domestic sources. The problem, it would seem, is not simply emotion, but emotion in a feminine or domestic context.

It could also be claimed that the hallmark of traditional soap opera is badly performed emotion: easy, cliched, intimacy without skill, or finesse. There is, after all, a joke about *Crossroads* which says it is 'the only show where the walls are more moving than the people'. The programme's status as generally acknowledged 'worst of the worst' of television, was demonstrated by an advertisement for video recorders from the hire firm Radio Rentals. The slogan ran 'It can take twelve episodes of *Crossroads* (If you can)'.

Crossroads's occasional deficiencies at the level of performance, direction and writing are in many ways a direct result of the low status which the traditional soap opera (and by implication, its audience) commands within the industry. The schedules on *Crossroads* are punishing in the extreme. Each week two hours of drama are prepared from scratch: Monday and Tuesday are script rehearsal days, Wednesday is for a technical run-through. On Thursday morning the first of four episodes is recorded. Episode two comes after lunch, with Friday devoted to taping episodes three and four. Throughout this process the facilities are as limited as the time: the sets are tiny, the rehearsal rooms shabby and unrealistic. Claire Falconbridge, who until recently played secretary Miranda Pollard, says 'Whatever the critics say, we achieve miracles in a small way. I've often thought it would be nice if we could put little Ceefax sub-titles underneath saying ''We're done this under duress — under the most amazing conditions we've managed to produce this much drama'' '.

Of course, *Crossroads* is not the only programme to be shaped by tight production constraints. All television, from 'quality' single plays to soap operas works with limited resources. How much resources are devoted to a given programme depends on its status within the industrial system of television. An examination of the changing priorities within that system can reveal a great deal about how television perceives its own role. It is illuminating, therefore, to examine the factors which lie behind the new-found respectability of soap opera as a genre.

In part, the new status of soap opera is a result of Channel Four's interest in popular drama, and its subsequent investment in the Liverpool-based soap opera *Brookside*. Although, as a programme on a minority channel, *Brookside* attracts audiences less than half of those for *Crossroads*, its production facilities are far superior.

Brookside was in many ways the offspring of producer Phil Redmond's school serial *Grange Hill*. As such it represents a widening out of soap from its original, mainly domestic and female concerns. Rather laddishly, Phil Redmond, the series' creator, says 'Drama is not just knocking off the woman next door and wondering if you are going to get caught. It's wondering whether you are going to be able to pay the bills at the end of the week and whether the car will pass the MOT'. The series has managed to successfully introduce young characters, always a problem for television, and has a clear commitment to left-of-centre politics. It tries to deal with explicitly political issues, such as unemployment, in a way which goes beyond the nostalgic 'Hoggartian' working class world of *Coronation Street*. To give just one example, *Brookside* actor Ricky Tomlinson, who plays shop steward Bobby Grant and was himself

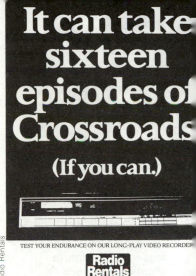
71

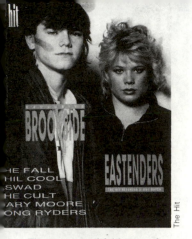

The new, youthful image of soap opera: the teenage magazine The Hit gets the stars of Brookside and EastEnders to give their verdicts on their rival series.

jailed for union activities in the early 1970's, said 'I wouldn't be doing this if it didn't face issues. People are going to find themselves confronted with all kinds of things that they never expect to see on *Coronation Street*'.

But *Brookside* is most clearly separated from previous British soap operas by its powerful, complex male characters and masculine stories. Men like Bobby, Barry and Damon Grant and Billy Corkhill are very different from the gentlemanly heart-throbs of *Crossroads*. A large number of *Brookside's* plots centre on these men, and their desires and aspirations. For instance, the heart of the recent storyline about fourteen year old Tracey Corkhill's affair with her teacher was her father's anguish: her own, and her mother's traumas rather took second place. Billy Corkhill, in fact, bears more than a passing resemblance to *Saturday Night and Sunday Morning's* Arthur Seaton, who does, after all end up moving to a new estate at the end of that film...

EastEnders marks the BBC's triumphant change of heart about soap opera. The opulent sets (at the old Elstree studios, purchased for the programme) large cast, and greater financial resources available to the production, represent the most advanced stage in the rehabilitation of the genre and illustrate just how much the BBC's attitude towards the popular audience has shifted. The *EastEnders* men are as complex as any of those in *Brookside*, but the series also has tough women, much more clearly in the mould of traditional soap opera: for instance, Angie, who runs Albert Square's pub, the Queen Vic, has clear similarities with Bet Lynch, now the landlady of The Rover's Return. All the same, it is interesting to wonder whether *EastEnders* would have been given the status, facilities and massive backing of the BBC without *Brookside's* temporary de-feminisation of the genre and it's consequent newfound respectability.

ALL THE CLASSICS

Throughout the fifties and early sixties a surprising number of middle-class families deliberately chose not to buy the new equipment capable of receiving ITV. Some even sought out the old BBC-only sets, presumably as a hedge against 'barbarism' and Americanised 'vulgarity'. The audience's perceptions of the channels have shifted little since then. The majority of viewers still see the BBC as the station of the middle classes ('the one the Queen would watch', according to one viewer), and believe ITV to be for the working classes. These images are so strong that programmes which do not conform to them are often misattributed: a recent IBA survey found that 39% of viewers believed the 'quality' hit *Brideshead Revisited* to be a BBC production, while 42% thought it was ITV which transmitted the glossy American soap *The Thorn Birds*.

With rare exceptions television's 'stodgy wedge' of popular programming (as one critic evocatively called it) is not something to be discussed in polite society. Popular television, and the pleasure it offers, is often hidden away rather like a dark secret, a source of lies and distortions. Soon after the news of Elsie Tanner's sudden departure from *Coronation Street*, *The Guardian* carried a front page cartoon which showed a woman complaining to her husband that 'The trouble with pretending never to have watched Coronation Street is that when something like this happens you can't talk about it'.

As far as many critics in the quality press are concerned popular television is a largely off-bounds netherworld, best observed at arm's length. An article on sit-com by *The Telegraph* critic Sean Day-Lewis begins with the preamble 'For the second of my expeditions into television areas usually neglected by reviewers...' Note the use of the word 'expedition': it sounds as though he is about to set foot in a treacherous, snake-infested jungle. Chris Dunkley, the TV critic of *The Financial Times*, has an almost anthropological approach to soap opera viewers. He says 'with such a large percentage of the population watching (soap operas) it seems reasonable to have a look (at them) every few years — not as drama, but as curious social phenomena'.

This kind of incomprehension is based not simply on a dislike for such programmes in themselves. From Orwell to those currently worried by *Dallas* this critical distaste is backed up by the uncomfortable knowledge that the forms of entertainment they dislike are massively popular. Many writers share an unspoken assumption that quality inevitably implies a minority audience — and that anything which is really popular must be bad.

Bryan McAllister

"The trouble with pretending never to have watched Coronation Street means that when something like this happens you can't talk about it."

Consequently, 'respectable' hits from popular genres are not often used as examples of just how interesting popular television can be. Instead, their similiarities to other popular programmes are often downplayed. When *Coronation Street* started earning accolades from then Poet Laureate John Betjeman, the majority of critics ignored its relationship with other soap operas like *Emergency Ward 10*. These rather lowly connections were dwarfed by references to 'the Dickens tradition'.

From the very beginning, British television has always had something of a fixation with high culture. In 1930, when Baird was still in the process of convincing a recalcitrant BBC of television's importance, his most ambitious broadcast was a play: Pirandello's *The Man With The Flower in His Mouth*. In the two and a half years following 1936, the BBC produced a total of 326 plays including works by Shakespeare, Sheridan, Shaw and Synge. There was a good deal of ballet and opera on early TV: far more in fact, than can be seen on television nowadays. Until 1954, an entire evening's viewing each year was pre-empted for live Glyndebourne opera.

Frilly costumes and stately homes in two landmark classic serials: The Forsyte Saga **and** Brideshead Revisited.

BBC-2

Nearly twenty years after Baird's test runs, the pattern was repeated by another new television service keen to prove itself: ITV. Though they swiftly moved on to Hughie Green and **Double Your Money**, their first night begun with Sir John Barbirolli and the Halle Orchestra. Today, the same nervous retreats into the realms of 'art' can be observed amongst the ITV companies when their franchises are due for renewal by the IBA. Whenever television institutions are in doubt about their status, they tend to run for the cover of older, more established arts, almost as though it were possible for them to gain respectability by association.

This tendency is aggravated by the way that television tends to be seen as something which is at its best when 'transmitting' other art forms rather than as a cultural medium in its own right. John Reith, the patrician father of the idea of public service broadcasting, saw the transmission of classical music, serious West End plays, educational programmes and scholarly talks as the central aim of radio. For Reith, radio was a transparent medium, relaying the life-blood of knowledge to those who would not otherwise have had access to it: allowing the 'crofter in his croft and the labourer in his squalid tenement' to sit side by side with the theatre patron in the stalls.

Reith's television heirs continued to hark back to many of these same ideas. The emphasis is still very often on sound instead of pictures and on accurately relaying other arts, rather than on the imaginative resources of television itself. Writing about classic serials on television, Mike Poole says 'purists would argue that... the only legitimate function of an adaptation (of a book) is to ghost the original. But of course, once such an approach is adopted it becomes impossible to evaluate the finished product in anything other than literary terms. The question becomes not ''what kinds of use does it make of the book'', or even ''what kind of television results'', but ''simply is it true to its origins?'' And in this sense, adaptations are just another instance of the way television consistently works to conceal the kind of construction being put on the material it presents'.

74

Perhaps the clearest recent example of this tendency was the BBC's adaptation of Scott Fitzgerald's **Tender is the Night**. In a newspaper advertisement for the programme (revealingly, this programme was chosen to break with the old BBC policy of not advertising) there was a strong emphasis on the fact that the book had been adapted for TV by Dennis Potter, who has some of the most impressively tele-visual plays ever made for British television under his belt. And the symbol used for Potter? A quill pen — possibly the most facile symbol of literary respectability imaginable.

A quick survey of what is normally considered most prestigous suggests that 'good television' is actually 'good something else': 'good art', 'good scholarship', 'good theatre'. When a programme is praised,

Channel 4

the implication is often that it has been so successful it has transcended its humble, technological origins as television.

British culture still has a heavy investment in believing certain arts to be 'pure' of the taint of trade. Those artistic forms which can't be separated from the baleful influence of industry tend to be consistently undervalued: witness the snobbery which still surrounds areas like industrial design. As Mike Poole notes, a quick survey of the backgrounds of past and current critics shows a peculiarly inappropriate bias towards the literary and theatrical establishment. Current 'literary men' installed as TV critics include the poet Hugo Williams (*New Statesman*), theatre critic Herbert Kretzmer (*Daily Mail*) and the novelists Peter Ackroyd (*Telegraph*) and Julian Barnes and Martin Amis (*Observer*).

Productions which can claim an association with the literary establishment, are especially highly regarded. Above all, it is the literary adaptation which has come to represent the most central component of 'good television'. *The Forsyte Saga*, *The Pallisers*, *David Copperfield*, *Sons and Lovers*, *Pride and Prejudice*, *Brideshead Revisited*, *Nicholas Nickleby*, *The Jewel in The Crown*, *Bleak House*, ...the list of productions goes on forever, each one a tribute to television's great love affair with books. And a certain type of British literature in particular: that which clearly signals its 'Englishness', not only in the nationality of original authors, but in the BBC's tradition of carefully authenticated costumes and props and its lavish use of landscape especially with stately homes.

An additional key factor here lies in the way classic serials, like single plays, have an apparently identifiable 'author', while most popular television programmes do not. Television critics are hampered by the long running Western tradition, in which art of all sorts is valued especially highly when it can be seen as the product of a solitary, (and ideally tortured), individual genius.

For most television arts programmes, John Wyver writes 'biography is paramount, as is the personal testimony of the artist'. There is a rock hard conviction that 'the artist's *personal* biography, related in individualist terms, will always be revealing about the work... and that work will benefit from being understood in relation to biographical attitudes and anecdotes': hence the popularity of the studio interview, the filmed profile, and the life reconstructed through personal photographs, excerpts from diaries and interviews with friends.

This approach serves television very badly. In the world of TV clearly identifiable 'authors' who could be said in the classical way to be inspired with a personal vision of genius are thin on the ground. And the simple reason for that is that, with the exception of the small scale area of avant-garde work often described as 'artist's video', television, as we have seen in the areas of *Crossroads* and *EastEnders*, is a collaborative and industrial medium. Only a minority of television programmes can be easily attributed to a single mind. Just who was responsible for the power of *Edge of Darkness*? Troy Kennedy Martin, who wrote the series? Director Martin Campbell, architect of the visual style so crucial to the programme's resonance? Or Michael Wearing, BBC producer previously known for his work on *The History Man* and *Boys From the Blackstuff*, overseer of the project as a whole? Or was it Ron Peck, the relatively inexperienced television actor who played detective Ronald Craven and became the most publicly visible face of the series?

These are some of the problems raised in trying to use a classical artistic approach to look at a short series, the total length of which was only six hours. These problems are magnified when we try to deal with the most typical of television's forms, long running series and serials.

BBC-1

BBC-2

Male dilemmas in The Boys From the Blackstuff **(left) and** Edge of Darkness **(right). Would similar programmes with female stars be as successful and as critically acclaimed?**

The credit for the original conception of *Minder* clearly goes to Leon Griffiths, but what was his role in the dozens of episodes written entirely by other people? Can any one person be celebrated as the single 'author' of 25 years of *Coronation Street* that have accumulated on the shelves of Granada television? How does a critic whose points of reference are the condensed, handleable models of discrete films and plays even begin to think about something that has run for more than a thousand hours, and been directed, produced, written and acted by a whole regiment of different people?

Some critics, taking their cue from the 'auteurist' approach to cinema developed in the fifties and sixties, have tried to challenge the low status of television by searching for individual 'authors'. Trevor Griffiths, (author of *The Comedians*, *Bill Brand*, and *Country*...), David Mercer (*In Two Minds*, *Shooting the Chandelier*...), Stephen Frears (*Bloody Kids*, *Saigon: Year of the Cat*...), Roger Graef (verite documentaries from *The Space Between Words* to *Police*) and Dennis Potter (*Pennies From Heaven*, *Blue Remembered Hills*...) have all been singled out for personal acclaim.

In the same way the current 'rehabilitation' of soap opera has coincided with the discovery of 'authors' for the programmes. From the beginning of the serial producer Phil Redmond was clearly identified with *Brookside* as a personal vision. Around the same time, a similiar process was underway at *Coronation Street*. Whereas for many years no one figure had clearly been identified as the author of the series, in recent years Tony Warren (the original creator and script consultant) has started to become the public face of the series. The programme celebrating twenty-five years of *Coronation Street*, itself a sign of the changing fortunes of the genre, placed Warren clearly as the 'creator' of the characters.

The attempt to ascribe a single point of origin to television programmes such as these downplays the extent to which all television production is a complex industrialised procedure, involving various types of constraints, routines and standardised working methods. Whether we are concerned with soap opera or classic serials, it is important to recognise that each are produced according to particular, though different, rules.

In fact, the pleasures offered by these series are often quite similiar to those offered by other, less respectable, parts of television. The visual pleasures offered by *Miami Vice* and *Brideshead Revisited* are different: one is to do with speed and the 'Americanised' look of neon, the other focusses on more langorous, pastel colours. The costumes have separate class connotations, the lighting a different look. One production is clearly marked out as British while the other has all the hallmarks of Americana so despised by Orwell and Hoggart. To compare them as pieces of television, however, it is not enough to fall back on those cultural ideas drawn from traditional art criticism whether from the knot of beliefs and prejudices which form the heart of anti-Americanism, a disdain for 'feminised' genres or an obsesson with clearly authored forms. The challenge is to develop a form of television criticism that can make sense of the particular forms of pleasure which the medium offers, in its popular programmes as much as anywhere else.

Max Headroom/Channel 4

PEOPLE WHO TELL YOU THINGS

Television employs endless people to tell us things: they tell us the news, the weather, the sports scores. They tell us about paintings, buildings, animals, everyday events, international crises. We learn the rules in game shows from them and the time of day and what is coming up next after the programme. Presenters come in many styles: like dog owners at Crufts we are adept at recognising the different breeds. We can distinguish the collar and tie-d seriousness of newsreaders from the dungareed idiocy of the hosts on children's programmes and pop shows. We realise 'gurus' like David Attenborough and Jonathan Miller will offer a very different style of programme from 'men of the people' like Terry Wogan.

Viewers also understand the protocol associated with presenters. We know that some of them smile, while others don't; that newsreaders are not allowed to wave their arms around, while such gestures are obligatory for Magnus Pike. In fact, we are so well versed in the rules that many of them have become invisible: we only become aware of them when they are broken. Television comedians have not been slow to capitalise on the comic potential of this situation. From **Q5** through to **The Two Ronnies, Monty Python's Flying Circus, Victoria Wood on Television** and Saturday Night Live, comedy has thrived on the ploy of twisting the normal forms of presentation. The occasions when real presenters deviate from expected behaviour provide another source of television humour, as viewers of **It'll Be Alright on the Night** know. It is a revealing illustration of the strictness of the codes that the simple sight of a newsreader fluffing a line, gargling or eating a chicken leg is treated as a cause for hilarity.

When they are not amusing us by getting it wrong, the presenter's role is that of a guide. They lead us from one television experience to the next, encouraging us to follow them to 'another part of the studio' or 'out to the scene of the action'. Presenters direct us through the material as well, telling us what is important and what should be ignored. They enforce order rather like old-fashioned, upper-class nannies, briskly sweeping chaotic masses of facts, people and events into neatly arranged sequences.

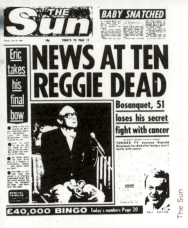

The private lives (and deaths) of public figures. Newsreaders may not write the news, but they have come to make it themselves with increasing frequency.

The maintenance of continuity is the other slightly nannyish task performed by presenters. We saw in the second chapter that the continuousness of television is an essential aspect of the viewer's relationship with the medium: presenters are the glue that holds television together. They are the guardians of television's 'flow', integrating disparate segments of television into a coherent evening's viewing. In *Grandstand* it was the presenter's job to weld a whole series of different sports into a single programme. Variety shows, meanwhile, use presenters to smooth the transition between the musical number, the magician and the comedy routine. It was our knowledge of the occasional absurdities of this juggling act which made *Monty Python's* cod presenter's link 'And now for something completely different…' into such a telling catchphrase.

The presenter's linking role does not end with each individual programme, however: a successful practitioner must establish continuity over periods of months and even years. On current affairs programmes like *Newsnight* and *First Tuesday*, the studio commentators have to forge a regular event out of a mass of separate reports which may have widely different styles.

Continuity presenters are required to keep the show on the road in an even more extreme fashion by tying different programmes together. John Wyver writes that 'No matter that a sequence of programmes may embrace sexist comedy and feminist polemic, the disturbing harshness of current affairs and the caressing cosyness of a costume drama. Insert a single voice, a reassuring script and similar title cards between each programme and all the contradictions and conflicts are quickly resolved'.

Viewers build up an easy, almost neighbourly familiarity with the presenters who come so regularly into their homes. Their names, faces, and mannerisms (Patrick Moore's blink, Michael Parkinson's ear-pulling) become as everyday as those of the viewer's families. Moreover, the presenters' insistent presence gives viewers the impression that they know them as people even when they may be doing jobs, like newsreading, which offer remarkably little personal data. Some viewers feel close enough to 'their' presenter to make personal comments about his or her clothes, pronunciation and state of mind: witness, for example, some of the letters to the tabloid newspapers. Neither are viewers shy about making irritable, even vitriolic, denunciations of certain personalities.

The conviction that the figures on television are 'real', knowable individuals rather than carefully managed and groomed images, is exaggerated by the interest of newspapers and magazines. The increasing tendency for print journalism to 'piggy-back' on the popularity of television's fictional stars (see chapter two) extends to the presenters who find themselves the subjects of stories with headlines like 'Anna Ford Speaks for Herself' and 'Me and My Privacy by Selina Scott'. The scandals surrounding Reginald Bosanequet's divorce and Anna Ford's wine throwing made front page news.

Characteristically, this publicity stresses the interchangability of the presenter's public performance and the reality of their off-screen lives. Writers struggle to merge the two pictures into one coherent whole, even when the story suggests a distinct gap between public and private lives — such as the tabloid features on the antique collection of *The Price is Right's* host Leslie Crowther. These feelings of intimacy are related to the role television presenters perform for their viewers. Often, they appear to act as mediators, occupying a curious position half way between the sitting rooms of those watching and the experiences which are being shown on television. Their 'invitations' imply they can help us to enter otherwise obscure worlds. On documentaries they point out things we might miss; on talk shows, they introduce their famous guests to us.

This convention is exaggerated by the presenter's language, especially their use of an inclusive we. The presenter may say '*we* are going to talk to x': in reality they mean *they* are going to have the conversation while we eavesdrop. A similarly bizarre convention lies behind the tag lines of many presenters of light entertainment. It was all very well for Bruce Forsyth to proclaim 'Nice to see you; to see you nice' on *The Generation Game* but obviously he couldn't *see* the viewers at all. The same, of course, applies to all those hosts who sign off by saying 'see you next week'.

The most important device in this relationship, however, is that of *direct address*. Interviewees, especially ordinary members of the public are not usually shown looking directly at the camera. It is only presenters who can regularly 'catch the camera's eye' and stare at the viewers, a strategy which makes those watching feel they are being personally addressed.

The invention of the auto-cue — a machine which reflects the words printed on a roll of paper onto a mirror in front of the camera — helped to strengthen the ritual of direct address. Skilled use of this machine allows the presenter to speak continuously without looking down from the camera to consult notes. The smooth, fluent diction which results tends to give an intense impression of interest and knowledge, even if the presenter is simply parrotting words they don't understand. After all, anyone who can read can explain the theory of relativity with the help of an auto-cue.

CHANGING THE NEWS

News is supposed to be the most truthful and objective part of television: a status which means it is especially important in television's image of itself. It could be argued that the point at which television took over the newspapers as the main source of the population's news marked an important shift in the role of the medium. The presentation of news is therefore of utmost importance for television institutions. Indeed, it often seems that there is a direct link between the authoritativeness of television channels, and the authoritativeness of their news presenters.

Krishan Kumar has written, for instance, that during the early years of the BBC, Reith used a particular style of presenter as part of his attempt to make the BBC into a distictive national institution. 'It is striking' Kumar says 'that from the very start Reith and his senior staff adopted a deliberate policy of using the announcers to create ''the public image'' of the BBC. ...They were intended to create a particular style by which the BBC could be identified in the public mind, and which more than any other device was to be used to establish a special moral and cultural authoritativeness'. Announcers were supposed to be the living incarnation of the BBC, with formality and seriousness as their keynotes: until the war, dinner jackets were required dress even for radio announcers.

Dinner jackets may no longer be necessary, but television institutions still try to closely identify newsreaders with the 'style' of their particular channel. The newsreader must embody the authority of the programme they appear in. They have to make the news seem neutral: something commonsense and obvious. In this country, news is often presented as something which simply lies there waiting to be 'found ' by eager reporters. In actual fact; the news, like the rest of television, is the result of careful processes of selection and editing. Prevailing ideas of 'newsworthiness' will deem some stories important, and others less so. Some people will be seen as crucial interviewees: others will be defined as less reliable, or less interesting and their opinions will not be sought with such ardour. For instance, the statement of a black South African liberation group may either be seen as a peripheral side-issue to a hanging in Pretoria or as a vital part of a story, depending on the frameworks of newsworthiness which are dominant within a department. None of these complexities will be visible in the programme itself: instead, it is the job of the newsreader to present the news as an objective truth.

A whole series of intensely ritualised conventions have emerged to shore up the authoritativeness of the newsreader. Aside from the steady, style of auto-cue direct address, there are the title sequences. Some of these draw on long established symbols of authority, such as **News at Ten**'s use of Big Ben. Others, such as the BBC's revamped **Nine O'Clock News**, use images of high technology and science: motifs which signal precision and neutrality. With rare exceptions, such as some of the BBC's old off-peak bulletins and TV-am's early morning programme **Daybreak**, the paraphernalia of the newsroom is kept well hidden. Newsreaders are seen sitting sedately behind austere and un-

cluttered desks — a classic symbol of importance.

It is usually assumed that the most desirable tone of voice for reading the news is a moderate, assured, reasoned one. Intonations which might suggest specific, personal interpretations of the material being read are, for the most part, carefully shunned: 'correct pronunciation' and a 'classless accent' are much sought after. An article by Stuart Marshall puts these characteristics in a rather different light. 'Mispronunciation' he says, can be seen as 'individual pronunciation — an assertion of an individual's history. The classless accent', he says, is in fact 'a middle class accent which has become so naturalised as to appear ''classless'' or normative. These extraordinary intonation patterns represent a kind of violence done to the voice in order to subdue all individual characteristics and emotive responses. ...The sum total of these qualities is a concentration upon what is said rather than how it is said.' Above all, what counts is 'the production of the voice as the voice of authority': nothing about the voice must jar or distract or suggest that any other interpretation of the material is possible.

The same kind of restrictions surround the newsreader's body. Unlike Michael Parkinson, who used to be shown tripping down his famous stairs, or Kenneth Clark who strolled in front of buildings, newsreaders are never seen to 'arrive' on the scene. They are there, ready and waiting, when the programme begins. And they don't move once the programme starts, either. Although at the beginning of ITN newscasters used to be seen out on location on filmed reports, nowadays they are firmly rooted to their chairs: a convention which added flavour to the tabloid's lewd discussions about the shape of Angela Rippon and Anna Ford's legs. In fact, for most of the time, only the newsreader's heads and shoulders are seen. Stuart Marshall suggests that this 'denial of the body' is necessary because 'the body is notoriously wayward in its capacity to communicate. Far too frequently it can undermine, even contradict the message of the voice'. These dangers are circumvented by confining the newsreader to a desk, and giving them a surface behind which to hide their hands.

The newsreader has to 'orchestrate' a whole series of other images and less authoritative speakers. Partly this is done with the aid of the codes of direct address: by momentarily turning to them the newsreader can 'pass' their 'look' to someone else, thus 'allowing' them to speak directly to the camera. For instance, in a two-handed broadcast a newsreader may turn to his or her companion, signalling that they are now the proper focus for the viewer's attention. Alternatively, they may look at an in-vision monitor, where a reporter is about to begin speaking from an outside location.

The American term for a newsreader — the 'anchor' — carries evocative connotations of a safe, secure coupling in a turbulent sea. In a newsworthy world of drama and crisis, newsreaders provide a secure, fixed point. It is telling, for instance, that Peter Sissons, the presenter of **Channel Four News** describes his job in terms of 'holding things down'. An article by John Langer suggests there may also be a visual component to this role: he notes that the newsreader's head and shoulders are always shown 'balanced and central in glistening, unwavering focus'. This, he suggests is a powerful contrast to images of the 'real' world of location news reports, which is 'often skewed, off balance, with shaky camera work done in the heat of the moment'. Reporters may sweat, look worried and duck bullets 'out there', but inside the studio all is calm. Implicitly, newsreaders offer the possibility of a safe resolution to the moments of tension and disaster they tell us about. They have to be a reassuring presence suggesting that while chaotic scenes may happen elsewhere, life 'at home' goes on as normal.

These routines and rituals are so well established that they ensure massive personal authority for the individuals concerned as well as for the news itself. As the public face of the news, presenters give the appearance of power: for those watching, this is easily interpreted as real influence. Curiously, the apparent omnipotence of newsreaders means that viewers also tend to drastically over-estimate newsreaders actual *presence*. It is surprising to find that even at the height of Anna Ford's fame she was rarely on screen for more than 3 minutes a night.

Newsreaders can become highly regarded pundits whose attitudes are canvassed on a variety of different issues. When they cease to read the news, and are freed from BBC contracts or IBA regulations, they become highly sought after by advertising agencies. They have, after all, managed to gain authority from news: the advertisers hope that, in turn, some of that credibility will adhere to their products.

This applies even when the newsreaders have little power over the words they say, and are chiefly skilled at scanning an auto-cue and taking instructions. At the BBC, newsreaders often have a background as actors or performers, and are completely uninvolved in the process of newsgathering. Even at ITN, where newscasters usually have a background as reporters, they may have little actual input into the daily

84

A calm reassuring presence spanning the world? Smart and smiling, Julia Sommerville, John Humphries and Andrew Harvey pose with the globe on the BBC's new look Nine O'Clock News set.

BBC-1

decision making process which lies behind the words they speak.

Traditionally, the BBC has always been worried that the personal authority which becomes attached to presenters could make them appear to be speaking on behalf of themselves rather than the television institution: a fear which provides a useful insight into the ways television thinks about itself. Krishan Kumar suggests that in its earliest stages the BBC wanted to become an authoritative institution in its own right, venerated in the same abstract way as the Civil Service, the Law Courts and the colleges of Oxford and Cambridge. Accordingly, the authority of newsreaders was closely associated with the BBC itself. Newsreaders were supposed to speak as the voice of the institution incarnate: serious, constant, unemotive. A 1936 memo stated 'The BBC is one Corporation and can only be thought of by the listener as an individual. It has many voices but one mouth...It is a commonplace that ''all announcers sound alike''. That is a tribute to their training'.

These strictures survived well into the post-war period. Television news broadcasts fell under the severe guardianship of New Zealander Tahu Hole. He believed that the junior medium of television needed to be strictly subordinated to the conventions established by radio. Pictures were only permitted when handcuffed to the serious and respectable sense of sound: for many years all that Tahu Hole would permit was a sound-only reading of the late radio news, accompanied by a still photograph of Big Ben. Scoops and exclusives were frowned upon as undignified, and any hint of personality from the presenters continued to be rigorously supressed.

Grace Wyndham Goldie, later Head of Television Talks and Current Affairs, gives an accurate summary of the BBC point of view. 'The fear', she says, 'was that if news was personalised it would no longer be ''the news'', an anonymous statement of facts given with all the authority of a famous newspaper such as **The Times** or of a great organisation such as the British Broadcasting Corporation: it could seem the ''news according to'' the particular newsreader seen on the television screen, known by the public, liked or disliked, but essentially a fallible individual'.

In 1954, with ITV on the horizon, the BBC began **News and Newsreel**, a curious hybrid of a programme which attempted to combine the severity of radio news with the seemingly dubious news values of cinema newsreels. At first no newsreaders could be seen. Later, Tahu Hole relented — provided individuals were selected from Broadcasting House on a strict rota, regardless of their ability to communicate. The result, according to Grace Wyndham Goldie was 'pretentious, unattractive and lamentably amateurish'.

All this changed with the introduction of ITV, and the coming of ITN news. ITV's attitude to news was as markedly as different from the BBC's as its approach to light entertainment. Whereas the BBC saw itself as

taking culture to the people, ITV had a more populist conception of the televison audience. It liked to think of itself as being of the people and claimed its power came from its representation of viewers. While the BBC continually strove to become a monolithic, single entity, with its news devoid of personality, ITN wanted to be energetic and human.

The new programme made a clear decision to foreground individuals. It introduced personality newscasters, chosen for their skill at journalistic communication rather than for delivering official communiques. From ITN's perspective, personality was an aid to authoritativeness, rather than a problem. Peter Black quotes Robin Day, one of the first newscasters, as sayng 'the idea was that as the newscaster became known to his viewers, his professional grasp of the material and his interest in it would make news more authoritative and entertaining'.

The brief given to Robin Day and ex-MP and athlete Christopher Chataway, was to supply both responsibility *and* vigour. They were encouraged to avoid long formal words and to simplify turgid governmental statements. Peter Black suggests in his book on ITV that 'the exact quality that (editor Aiden Crawley) sought was captured perfectly one night when Chataway was reading an item about an athletics meeting:' Chataway said ''There goes my record for the five thousand metres. Tharos beat it by more than nine seconds''. The BBC soon introduced in-vision newsreaders of its own and began to see its role in a slightly more consensual, less patrician fashion. The regime of dinner jacketed radio announcers was giving way to the one which would encourage Angela Rippon to dance on **The Morecambe and Wise Christmas Show.**

The clearest example of the contrasting positions of BBC and ITV presenters comes from outside of the strict confines of the news broadcast. Although the BBC eschewed personality in the news, they were happy for it to flourish in other, less tendentious areas. Most of all, the BBC benefited from the close relationship that grew up between it and solemn, elder statesman presenter Richard Dimbleby. His son, reporter/presenter Jonathan Dimbleby has written that 'if Reith created the BBC, as was commonly said, then Dimbleby was its voice'.

In Dimbleby, the BBC at last found the identification between the BBC and the institutions of state that Reith had always hankered after. In particular, the popular acclaim heaped on Dimbleby's commentary for **The Coronation** suggested that an enduring link had been formed between the Corporation, the monarchy and, by implication, Britishness itself. According to Malcolm Muggeridge, Dimbleby was 'the goldmicrophone-in waiting': at his premature death a few years later, viewers wrote saying that 'It is as though a piece of England has gone' and 'Richard Dimbleby *was* BBC television'.

In contrast to the solemnity of Dimbleby, the public face of ITN belonged to a group of tough, meritocratic, young professionals.

Although the new men, like Robin Day, were as highly educated as their BBC rivals, they were 'grammar school boys' rather than old school tie aristocrats or Foreign Office types. Many of them were more interested in television for its own sake than some more Reithian notion of 'service'; to them Dimbleby's style of commentary verged on the bland and obsequious.

In a biography of his father, Jonathan Dimbleby compares the way Robin Day and Richard Dimbleby covered the 1958 State Opening of Parliament, the first royal occasion televised after the start of commercial television. Day's commentary was brisk, dry and efficient: Dimbleby's style its usual blend of lavish formality. Day opened by saying 'Well, it is a dull, damp morning': Dimbleby began 'It is a grey, rather still, misty day'. Day said: 'And down there the clump of dirty grey from the wigs of the High Court judges', while Dimbleby intoned: 'Now the cluster of judges in scarlet and ermine and black and gold take their places...' Dimbleby finished his commentary in classic style by saying 'The Throne remains — rich, shining — near yet remote — the symbol of this rare meeting of the Queen, the Lords and the Commons — the Three Estates of Parliament. And so begins, with ceremony that springs from the very roots of our democratic history, the fourth session of the three hundredth Parliament of the Realm'. Meanwhile, Robin Day closed with the rough debunking attitude typical of his early ITV personna: 'The Queen will go back to Buckingham Palace. The crown will go back to the Tower of London. All the scarlet and ermine robes will go back to wherever they came from. And Parliament will go back to work...Everyone is wondering at Westminster what government will write the next speech from this Throne. Before Her Majesty sits on it again there may be a General Election. That is when we have our say. And what Her Majesty reads from this throne depends on what we put in the ballot box'.

The new, more consensually based attitudes to authority developed by ITN and swiftly taken up by Hugh Greene's BBC, resulted in an enlarged role for personality in the news. But this still did not mean that presenters reflected a genuine cross-section of the population. The fact that television institutions were now trying to 'borrow' back authority from their presenters meant that newsreaders were, on the whole, drawn from those groups usually regarded as authoritative. Still, today, the overwhelming mass of newsreaders are middle-class, male and white. There are no network television newsreaders with marked regional accents, none with any visible disability and remarkably few women over the age of 40. Fran Morrison from **Newsnight** comments 'I'll believe women have really made it when they're allowed to age as disgracefully as the men on television'.

And yet, the democratic rhetoric of television has meant that certain changes in the social fabric must eventually be reflected in television's choice of presenters, and most especially, newsreaders. There is, for

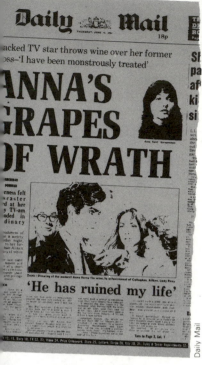

Newscaster as star: Anna Ford's public irritation with her ex-boss gets front page treatment by the Daily Mail.

instance, now a tiny nucleus of black newsreaders, fronted by Trevor McDonald and Moira Stewart. But in every other way, these newsreaders adhere rigidly to the long-established rules and regulations for neutral and impartial newsreading.

Although late in coming, middle-class black newsreaders were eventually absorbed into the definition of acceptably authoritative newsreaders. The history of how women newsreaders achieved such status is far more complex, involving a long-running and exceptionally public debate. The first women to read the news, Barbara Mandell (one of the early ITN newscasters) and Nan Wynton (who had a short-lived career as a BBC newsreader in 1960) were appointed against a background of argument about the appropriateness of the female voice. In 1961, for instance, a reporter on *The Observer* said that producers did not appoint women because 'When they become nervous their vocal chords tighten and their voices grow shrill...The class system divides women more strongly than men; men sound like men while women sound upper-class, or working class or suburban'. Apparently femininity was a bar to the requisite middle-class neutrality, regardless of the applicant's actual class position.

Behind the smokescreens of argument about the timbre of the female voice was a real concern that women lacked sufficient authority. In 1971, Radio Four's Head of Presentation was still seriously suggesting that no-one would believe a women if she announced the out-break of war. Women were seen as insufficiently qualified to contribute a calm centre between news items about social chaos. It *could* be argued, of course, that women's domestic life involves doing just that: juggling conflicting responsibilities while trying to appear calm. Similarly, Anna Ford argues that women's experience of domestic life is good training for coping with the contradictory demands that working in a studio places on the presenter.

Skills developed in the domestic sphere are rarely seen as having any relevance in the 'masculine' world beyond the home. It is interesting, however, that breakfast television is the one area of news coverage where women have come to be seen as an essential. This is the only type of news presented in a clearly 'domestic' manner: lounging chairs replace the desks, the men wear pullovers and the set resembles a sitting room. Even within a domestic environment, however, women can still be junior partners. As an article in *The Observer* pointed out, Selina Scott's 'on-screen relationship with Frank Bough resembles that between a young second wife and her more experienced husband'. The writer continues that 'a favourite word used for women presenters is "complementary". A successful female presenter tends to be one who is complementary to the already existing male, rather like Selina to Frank. Her gaucheness is often quoted in her favour, because it shows up Frank's professionalism — and of course, his niceness...'

Traditionally, recognition for women beyond the domestic sphere is connected with sexuality and physicality: areas which, as we have already seen, are taboo for authoritative newsreaders. Richard Ingrams from *The Spectator* voices such complaints in a typically provocative way by saying he doesn't like female newsreaders because 'Women are distracting. If they are pretty I can't concentrate on what they say, and if they are ugly I'm put off completely. Women are absolutely dreadful on television'.

Angela Rippon and Anna Ford were chosen to read the news by the BBC and ITN in the late seventies, a period when the social status of women was being hotly contested. Rippon and Ford became a focus for male uncertainty about the 'problem' of powerful, attractive women. Anna Ford, in particular, was discussed in a kind of sexy baby-talk: amongst other things she was dubbed a 'doe-eyed newscasterette' and the 'second news kitten'. The other tactic of the tabloids was the 'legs war', a hastily constructed rivalry between Angela Rippon and Anna Ford. *The Sun*, for instance, devoted a double page spread to 'Anna vs Angela'. The MP Tim Brinton and the paper's fashion and TV columnists were asked to give points in a competition to find 'Who's top for smile, style, eyes, thighs?' It is hard for a woman to be regarded as both intelligent and sexual: and, much as Anna Ford and Angela Rippon may have disliked the fact, they were discussed in a relentlessly sexual fashion.

By contrast, male sexual attractiveness is not ordinarily thought to detract from their authority. It did Michael Wood, the presenter of *In Search of the Dark Ages* and *In Search of the Trojan Wars*, no lasting harm to be described as possessing a 'passionate voice' and a 'lean bronzed physique', even if *Private Eye* ran a cartoon titled *In Search of a Tighter Pair of Jeans.* The televison companies which encouraged the wave of silliness surrounding Rippon and Ford and thrived on the ratings it produced were less certain about the development. The danger was not simply that they were seen as speaking personally, as Reith and Tahu Hole had feared. The real problem was that Rippon and Ford

At the height of the fame Angela Rippon and Anna Ford were subjected to an absurd 'contest' by The Sun.

were glamorous television *stars* whose popularity threatened to overwhelm the importance of the news itself. Since then, the publicity which television companies has given to their individual newsreaders has notably declined.

EXPERTS, AND ORDINARY PEOPLE

Experts like Kenneth Clark, A.J.P. Taylor, David Bellamy and Michael Wood are stars of a rather different kind. Rather than conflicting with their television role, these people use their personality to help make their subjects come alive. They are not representing the BBC or ITN, like

Being there, holding it: David Bellamy, **expert and man of the people shows off seaweed.**

newsreaders. But, neither do all of them simply speak for themselves. Many have links with institutions like universities: indeed this is part of their attraction for television. Reith wanted television to become an authoritative institution in its own right, a pillar of learning, able to stand alongside the most ancient of universities. It is a sign of television's uncertainty about its own role that the romance with such institutions has never entirely died. Television has constantly plundered prestigious institutions for presenters. From 1951 to 1959 a series of young ex-MP's (mostly Labour ones from Attlee's ousted 1945 government) were used as political commentators on programmes such as *International Commentary* and *India's Challenge*. There have also been academic historians like A.J.P. Taylor and scientists such as Mortimer Wheeler and David Bellamy. It could be argued that this involves the borrowing not only of expertise, but also of authority, much in the same way that fiction departments 'borrow' literary kudos through the classic serial: it is interesting, for example, that the credits of Bellamy's programmes were careful to list his academic credentials.

Some of the most extreme examples of this 'borrowing' of prestige comes in so-called guru series like *The Ascent of Man, Life on Earth, America* and *The Shock of The New*. Started by Kenneth Clark's *Civilization* these programmes emphasis the personality of an expert. to an almost absurd degree. This is foregrounded in interviews, reviews and photographs, particularly in *The Radio Times*, where such series are normally given the accolade of a front cover picture.

The growth of these series must also be related to the obsession of some areas of television with authorship, a factor, which as we saw, is of utmost importance in the classic serial. Many documentaries are structured around a desire to evaluate things in terms of a single source, a single consciousness. Think, for instance of the titles: *'James Burke's Connections*, *Wogan*, *Whicker!*, *Pilger* and *Parkinson*. Guru series like *Civilisation* and *America* announce themselves as 'personal' but their author's viewpoints fit more or less comfortably into the dominant, conventional view of what constitutes art, history, culture and so on. Just as the structure of news presentation helps to deny the decision-making process which lies behind it, so 'expert' documentary series tend to treat the ideas of their presenters as if they were absolute truth.

This is underlined by the way such series show their presenters standing in front of the objects they are talking about. Julian Petley writes that 'Constantly, the presenter is shown *in* the very places under discussion, *beside* the *actual* pictures or sculptures being analysed'...The press release for the *Civilisation* series enthused ''Two years to make. 80,000 miles covered. 200,000 feet of film shot — the equivalent of six major feature films. Eleven countries and 117 locations visited. Works in 118 museums and 18 libraries shown''.

In part these recitations are aimed at potential buyers: guru series make considerable income through foreign sales, and can attract large amounts of co-production money. But they also have a considerable impact on the viewer. 'Repeated again and again', Petley suggests, 'there is something almost mystical or metaphysical about this device: it's as if some kind of mythically conceived 'esence' of the original work of art, or the 'spirit' of the location might somehow flow magically through the presenter, camera and television screen and into our homes'.

In part, the power of these sequences is related to the phenomenon of tourism — the need to actually *visit* and see with one's own eyes places and objects of interest. Through the agency of the presenter we have the feeling that we too can feel immersed in the experience. Kenneth Clark may be a university professor but he is also someone

BBC-2

Much more sedate, though no less gripping, David Attenborough in Life on Earth.

Mr Universe

Jonathan Miller has the latest on the earliest moments in time in 'Origins', Tuesday BBC2. Inside: telling the old, old story, page 82

The full Radio Times treatment for 'Mr Universe' Jonathan Miller. Bathed in a pool of light, he could be a religious guru rather than a television one.

Serious quiz show Mastermind adds the trappings of documentary authority to the competition of the game show. Here, the host and contestants stand around the programme's most famous icon: the black leather chair.

standing in front of something, just in the way we could. Despite their carefully marketed academic status, the gurus speak personally: Kenneth Clark often begins by saying things like 'Every time I come here…' But, unlike any ordinary member of the public, the guru mixes these immediate, personal responses with knowlege — knowledge which we accept because it comes packaged with all the trappings of authority, the voice, the demeanour, the billing in the Radio Times.

Recently, the rather genteel image of Kenneth Clark standing in front of the building has become fused with the older-established entertainment tradition of having the presenter actually experience something. There is a direct line from 'being there and doing it' programmes like *Blue Peter* and *The Deep End* to David Bellamy; similarly, on *Life on Earth*, and *The Body in Question* Renaissance man Jonathan Miller subjects himself to electric shocks, sensory deprivation or acupuncture.

David Bellamy has a different style of address to that used by Jonathan Miller. Bellamy is boisterous and noisy, while Miller always mixes his enthusiasm with a certain composure. Miller is pure guru, but Bellamy's broken nose, unmistakable gutteral voice and propensity for flashy video effects mark him out as eccentric. In some ways, his performance is close to that of 'mad boffin' Magnus Pike, twitchy astronomer Patrick Moore and dog trainer Barbara Woodhouse: all favourites of television impersonators. These presenters are clearly obsessed by their subjects, but they also 'represent the people'. Even when they come from academic institutions, as Bellamy did, the manner of these eccentrics suggests that anyone with their special motivation could share their knowledge.

The relaxed, friendly demeanour of presenters like Bellamy is echoed in the development of styles of studio presentation which deliberately stress the *ordinariness* of the individuals concerned. Rather than simply trying to borrow their authority from the institution, like the early, anonymous BBC presenters, or being stars like Anna Ford, this other group of presenters claim to represent the viewer's interests by being 'one of the family' or 'just like them'.

As early as 1951 *Television Weekly* said that announcer Sylvia Peters and her co-workers were 'Part of the family circle. We feel we have only to stretch out our hands to touch them…This ability to be homely and friendly is, I think, a number one qualification for any TV announcer'.

It was, however, 1958 — when the BBC started *Tonight* to fill the 6 pm to 7 pm gap previously reserved for the 'toddler's truce' when mothers were supposed to put children to bed — that really marked the growth of the 'ordinary' presenter. Rather than employing the simple agenda for newsworthiness used by the news departments, these presenters hosted a programme which passed topical national issues through a filter of human interest, presenting the 'big' stories in terms of how they affected individuals. Entertainment items, such as the regular topical calypso, were mixed in with the more political stories in a previously unimaginable way. The mix suggested the disorganisation of 'ordinary' everyday life rather than the obsessive order of the news. Mistakes, when they occurred, were laughed off. Introducing the programme after the summer break in 1961 Cliff Michelmore said for example 'We are flippant, irreverent, disbelieving when we feel we should be; we refuse to be taken in by pompous spokesmen'. Most of all, however, *Tonight* claimed to speak on behalf of 'ordinary people' by the use of presenters who strived to be 'just like us'. Indeed, Grace Wyndham Goldie has said that 'If *Panorama* with Richard Dimbleby had become the voice of authority…*Tonight* with Cliff Michelmore…was the voice of the people'.

Even Alan Whicker, now established as a 'star', far more extra-ordinary than ordinary, was at the time seen as astonishingly direct and down-to-earth. Grace Wyndham Goldie says that 'Whicker, in his own way, was a representative of the ordinary man. He was as Baverstock (the programme editor) always intended the whole *Tonight* programme to be, clearly and obviously on the side of the audience. And he remained one of them. He never altered the kind of clothes he wore, or his tone of voice, whether he was interviewing a Master of the Quorn or a Paul Getty or a woman who believed in leprechauns'.

In contrast to the news, the image of *Tonight* was firmly domestic. The on-screen relationship between the presenters was shown as that of a 'television family': a family comparable, in fact, to those of the viewers at home. This was most clearly visible on the night when Cliff Michelmore's son was born, an event the programme treated in a way which suggested the excitement of friends and family rather than the careful seriousness of the news.

Nationwide was in many ways an up-dating of the *Tonight* formula. It had the combination of serious and entertaining items (described in the press as the 'disasters and skateboarding ducks' ethos), the cosy, first-name terms relationship between the presenters, and the same invitation for viewers to be part of 'a great big television family'. In their book on the programme Charlotte Brunsdon and David Morley say 'In *Nationwide* there is a thread of almost anti-intellectualism; 'experts' are held in some value for what they want to contribute, but it all has to be translatable into the language of immediate issues and everyday concerns…The team often expresses 'our' exasperation with politicians. Michael Barratt…presents himself as the embodiment of (a) 'populist' perspective: a no-nonsense man of the people, stressing common sense, not only by asking questions he thinks the public would want to ask, but…by adding comments ('Well, they do seem rather stupid reasons for going on strike…') he assumes the public might make, or at least agree with.'

The chatty style of *Tonight* and *Nationwide* is augmented by an alter-

Allan Whicker: A representative of the ordinary man?

native set of visual associations. Presenters are not always static behind their desks: they can be seen on location in reports and 'specials' and move around the studio. Rather than a supposedly neutral background, the studio becomes an environment. The desk starts being one of many elements in the studio, rather than the only item to be shown. The colours are different too. Whereas news programmes tend to stay with 'serious' blues and greys, 'family-style' programmes have their sets decorated in the range of colours a family might choose for a kitchen or living room: *Nationwide*, for instance, favoured pale yellow. Michael Barratt, the chief studio presenter, echoed this colour in his choice of suits and ties, something else unimaginable on a news programme.

On breakfast television the desk is dispensed with altogether. The set is deliberately dressed to resemble a sitting room, with sofas, coffee tables and flowers. Newspapers and coffee cups can be seen in front of the presenters: behind them at TV-am is a large, fake 'window' looking out onto trees. Casual clothes are worn: indeed Frank Bough's famous cardigans can be said to sum up the friendly face of the studiedly 'ordinary' presenter.

The desk itself may be the newsreader's prized status symbol, but it is little more than a trap for people in other parts of television. The hosts of youth programmes, who gain credibility through displays of anti-authoritarianism, go out of their way to treat their desks disrespectfully, sitting on them like trendy schoolteachers. Game show hosts, there to show enthusiasm and energy, are positively required to move around the studio. If they win, the contestants also get the chance to escape from their desks: in *The Price is Right* this escape takes the form of a 'promotion' from the desk-like 'staging post' of 'contestant's row' to the middle of the studio where the 'floor games' are played.

An exception to this rule, however, may be the respectable 'intellectual' game show *Mastermind*, a light entertainment programme which apes the trappings of authority normally associated with experts and newsreaders. Here the host, Magnus Magnusson, sits behind a desk. The slightly sadistic, inquisitorial style of questioning which is the trademark of the programme is underlined by the vulnerability of the contestant who sits, exposed, in a chair in a pool of light.

Despite their apparent differences, Magnus Magnusson, Leslie Crowther, David Bellamy, Jonathan Miller, Anna Ford, and Alastair Burnet all have equivalent jobs. Gurus, newsreaders and game show hosts are all there to transform otherwise disparate facts and activities into a coherent, intelligible whole.

Most important, they have to work within the boundaries established by their predecessors. They can play with the conventions, subtly modify them, even, in certain controlled circumstances, make gentle fun of them. But, for the majority of the time they must stick to the rules and play the game the way they are expected to.

REAL PEOPLE 5

The professional face of television is Robin Day, Leslie Crowther, Alastair Burnet, Selina Scott: abrasive political interviewers, smooth game show compères, personality presenters. There is, however, another less discussed group who also appear a great deal: ordinary members of the public. These individuals – rather revealingly described as Real People by some professionals – provide the substance of many of television's programmes. 'This is your show' Leslie Crowther tells the audience during his warm-up at *The Price is Right* 'without you there'd be no show'. The sentiment is echoed by documentary director David Cohen. 'I can't operate without real people. It'd be like making a feature film without actors'.

Countless documentaries, from *Man Alive* through to *World In Action* and *The Marriage*, are based around real people. They are the studio audiences for sit-coms, the missing persons who *Surprise, Surprise!* reunites with long lost relatives, the fanatical cat owners who enthuse about pet food in stop-a-person-in-the-street 'vox pop' commercials. Real people are the ones who question politicians on *Election Specials*, dance behind the professionals on *Top of the Pops*, eat brains while blindfolded on *That's Life*. Without them, television would just not look the same.

Although real people provide much of the content of much of what the television industry produces, they get few financial rewards for their contribution. In a business noted for its exceptional wages, real people alone belong to no union and receive derisory rates of pay. It is not unusual for a family to receive as little as £35 for a day's work on a networked documentary. Acknowledgement is often as limited as their pay: frequently they are just nameless bodies, undignified by a caption as they speak or any mention in the final credits. Real people are the uncelebrated and underpaid foot soldiers of non-fiction TV.

All the same, no-one in television wants real people to behave like the amateurs they are. When selecting them, directors pray for 'naturals': individuals who, without any rehearsal, can magically

95

conjure up skills that professionals spend years perfecting. An ideal real person will engage audiences by projecting a charismatic personality and talk in short sentences that are easily 'cuttable' by a film or video-tape editor. They will be good at understanding abstract hints from the production team and not mind waiting around for hours. Mike Russell Hills, director of countless vox -pop commercials for clients like Sainsburys and the Conservative Party, says 'the considerations are pretty much the same as if you were casting an actor or actress for the part, such as how outward are they, are they going to be easy to work with, do they look like they mean it?'

The reason directors like Mike Russell Hills don't take the easy way out and employ real professionals is simple: real people have qualities possessed by no actor, however astute. Eccentrics who populate programmes like *That's Life*, *People Are Funny* and *Game For A Laugh* are irreplaceable. The whole idea is that their 'human interest' stories exist in the awkward, unpredictable world outside the studio gates. With their talented performing pets and proclivity for building things out of matchsticks these people represent the peculiarly British idea that batty behaviour somehow equals 'all of human life'.

Although these 'cranks' are the heirs of a long established tradition going back through popular books and 30's radio, eccentrics had their television hey-day in the 50's with the original version of programmes like *People Are Funny* and *What's My Line*. Nowadays it is less fashionable to treat the working classes as though they are inherently amusing. The majority of television's 'civilians', as they are sometimes called, are less obviously flamboyant and quirky.

Real people are there to perform a specific task for television: most frequently, to illustrate an expert's thesis or the subjects of somebody else's show. Their words will be topped and tailed by the smooth phrases of an interviewer or light entertainment host. And real people do not usually get the chance to look directly at the camera. Instead, as we saw in the last chapter, they look at the professionals, who look at the camera for them, 'relaying' their expression to the people watching.

As 'examples', the real people have to communicate quickly and easily. A documentary protesting about poor housing needs people who appear to be visibly suffering from the conditions, not what looks like a comfortable, if frugal, household. Understandably, most professionals would shrink from using a voice-over to say that despite their neat and tasteful abode, the family on screen is actually very poor. In a similar way, Laurie Taylor, professorial real person, comments on the props vital for being 'academic' on

television. 'As soon as a crew arrives they always start looking for books: apparently a yard or so of books is essential. Once I was filmed in a rented flat and they went out especially to get some. The feminist writer Dale Spender sent me a postcard saying "I don't think we've met, but I know you've read my book – it was behind your head on your last TV appearance".'

The other part of the real person's job is to be just like those watching, to act as viewers momentarily whisked to the other side of the screen. They stand in for *us*, act as our representatives. They are our substitutes, approximating how we might feel as witnesses to a train crash on **The News**, or as the winners of a new kitchen on a game show. They provide us with a point of identification, offering a connection to events that might otherwise lack resonance. As documentary film-maker Caroline Pick says, 'If you want to touch viewers, make them interested in an issue, the obvious way is to find ordinary people who have been directly affected by that particular problem. The best way of pulling the viewer in is to get these people to sit there and talk about the experience in their own words'.

Mike Russell Hills and Caroline Pick need interviewees who will inspire empathy in the viewers by looking and sounding ordinary. Although a professional demeanour may help things go smoothly on the day of the shoot, the point of the exercise will be defeated if they end up looking like experts rather than members of the public. Real people are 'employed' to be ordinary. As Debbie Christie, a BBC producer, says, 'People can become professionals very quickly. Ironically, that 'party piece' approach can undermine the credibility of what they're saying'.

A certain roughness around the edges is one way round the problem of getting real people to look 'real'. Traits which would be handicaps for someone trying to become a professional news-reader can be assets to a real person: colourful clothes, slightly odd hair, shyness, expressive, personal speech patterns and even a touch of gaucheness, all provide a useful contrast to bland presenters. Regional accents are also highly valued by many directors: at one time, it seemed as though 'realness' only began north of the Midlands.

These characteristics are only a boon in small doses: too many idiosyncrasies make an interviewee look more like a mini-celebrity than an average, representative, viewer. Mike Russell Hills says that in selecting people for vox pops, 'It is not a matter of just going for the gushiest, pushiest person, because the biggest thing is their credibility. You musn't end up with someone who is so over the top that they won't come over as real. You can see the best ones having little games with themselves. They *say* "Oh, no, don't let it be me,"

but secretly they are all excited and can't wait to be stopped by the crew'. William G. Stewart, producer of **The Price Is Right**, chooses along the same lines: 'I wouldn't pick someone to be a contestant who would attempt to be a star. I want nice ordinary people who just come along for a bit of fun: some of them are so ordinary they are surprised to be chosen'.

'Nice ordinary' people are useful because they allow television to dwell on the small specificities of life. Real people excel at detail: at telling the moving anecdote which brings home the enormity of a war or strike, at expressing their feeling for cats and dogs in a few lines of a pet-food advertisement. They contribute a feeling for the ragged texture of real life – something vital for television.

Television's most popular programmes – soap operas, sit-coms and chat-shows – all emphasise everyday rather than extra-ordinary experiences. TV offers us figures whose heads are an equivalent size to our own and whose lives and emotions have much in common with ours. We can sit in our own sitting rooms doing the ironing, glancing at people who do the same kind of things as we do and speak the same kind of words as us. **The Marriage** didn't get its remarkable ratings with high-tech action or cinematic-scale passions and tragedies. Instead, the series, which traced a young Welsh couple's first year of married life, lingered (relentlessly, some unimpressed viewers might say) on the everyday details of their lives – arguments with building societies, worries about money, phonecalls to friends and petty infidelities.

Television is not in the business of mimicing the lives of those watching. Rather than striving to present a completely accurate (and probably boring) image of what ordinary life is actually like, television likes to celebrate the everyday: to show ordinary life writ large.

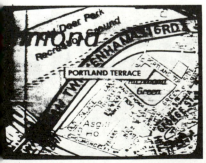

Marc and Karen Jones, the couple in question, were not destined to remain unknown. Instead, the a-typical amount of time and obsessive care which the BBC had lavished on their stunning ordinariness resulted in fame. Post-**The Marriage**, their presence was demanded on chat shows and their lives were avidly discussed in the tabloid press. When the theme tune for the series moved into the charts, Marc and Karen featured in a **Top of the Pops** video. Briefly, they were stars. But not glamorous Hollywood stars, surrounded by the trappings of other-worldly wealth. While **The Marriage** was showing they became quintessential television stars: extra-special versions of typical viewers. People who get plucked from the street to test margarine, comment on a current crisis or take part in a pratical joke don't experience any fanfare of personal publicity. The underlying premise, however, can still be seen as a celebration of the ordinary.

The apparent democracy of the vox pop goes very deep into television's view of itself. From Reith's early mission to bring all of life to the hearths of 'the masses', to Channel Four's contemporary video box, television has always wanted to believe that it is 'on the side' of the viewers, against cant and hypocrisy. It likes to think it is the heir of magazines such as *Picture Post*, aggressively militant on the part of the loser at one moment, able to laugh at the foibles of famous and ordinary folk alike at the next.

As William G. Stewart greets the cheering audience to *The Price is Right* he gives a graphic illustration of these attitudes. 'Welcome,' he shouts to the strains of Land of Hope and Glory, 'this is people's television.' Desmond Wilcox makes comparable claims for his 60's documentary series *Man Alive*. According to him, this was ground breaking, in showing 'ordinary people as flawed and credible for the first time, individuals just like you and me.' Wilcox's version of 'people's television' yields programmes a million miles from those created by William G. Stewart, but the master of the game show and the mentor of the emotional documentary both believe in careful use of members of the public. This, they feel, allows television to speak for, and celebrate, 'the people' as a whole. 'the people' as a whole.

GETTING EMOTIONAL

When directors cast real people they are looking for individuals who can bring a certain amount of warmth, personal passion and, most of all, emotion, to what they are saying. Whereas career presenters nurture their reputations for smoothness, control and unflappability, real people get points for playing the opposite role. They have to be skilled at communicating feelings – not holding them back like the professionals. Real people get excited and act spontaneously. They laugh hysterically, are willingly made fools of and let themselves appear as shocked or astounded or struck dumb with embarrassment. In the midst of tragedy they weep without shame. They are allowed, and often positively encouraged, to lose control of themselves.

Real people's emotions, passions and happiness provide a central part of the pleasure audiences get from game shows. Viewers told Laurie Taylor and Bob Mullan that they enjoy the spectacle of 'lots and lots of very happy – and sometimes quite ecstatic – people'. As Laurie Taylor later explained, 'There's something very pleasant about watching other people's enthusiasm. It's the same reason people love watching football crowds, and people jumping around on *Top of The Pops*. People who watch

the shows love the euphoria of all these people. Everyone having a wonderful time: that's what they like'. This corresponds closely to the utopian pleasures of 'energy' and 'intensity' described by Richard Dyer in his essay on how entertainment offers emotion experienced 'directly, fully, unambiguously, "authentically", without holding back.'

Certainly, these are desirable characteristics for participants in game shows. A winning application form to the *Crosswits* game show gives an almost perfect description of a real person: 'I am 57, a talkative, articulate, competitive, extrovert, outgoing, young and fat crossword puzzler'. Even more directly, viewers interviewed by Laurie Taylor and Bob Mullan said they preferred contestants with

Compere Leslie Crowther stays calm, but the best contestants are passionate, spontaneous and even a touch hysterical.

the 'ability to let themselves go mad'.

The same uninhibited skills stand real people in good stead for other parts of television too. Some of the most electrifying moments of 'serious' non-fiction TV come when people lose control, shouting at their bosses, pleading with their jailers, angrily demanding justice from police or pickets. There are also quieter, but no less emotional *frissons* to be had when real people bare their souls to the camera. Game shows give us the chance to be vicarously involved in someone else's euphoria. Documentaries, meanwhile, often offer a different form of intensity: the bitter-sweet intimacy which comes from hearing someone tell their darkest, unhappiest secret. Vivid, unqualified feeling is the keynote to both types of performance. Whether they are on *The Price is Right* or *40 Minutes*, the real person's job is to heighten and engage the emotions of those watching.

The pivotal moments of spectacle in 'gag' shows like *Candid Camera*, *Game For A Laugh* and *People are Funny* occur when the fall-guy realises what has happened and has to fight a battle (ideally an unsuccessful one) to stay in control of himself. When the contestant spots his wife coming onto the stage of their local club dressed as a stripper, as once happened in *Game For A Laugh*, the viewers get the chance to see naked confusion and panic. At the very least, the director hopes to be able to show someone forgetting that they are on television, 'acting naturally', in a spontaneous way. That instant, underlined with a close-up, reprised in an action-replay and spiced up by the replacement of minor expletives with 'bleeps', is the orgasmic point of the whole programme.

Surprise, Surprise! alternates these robust assaults on the composure of its contestants with gentler thrills provided by unexpected reunions. Old friends, estranged members of the family, people who saved the contestant's life in the war, or when they were a child, are collected together in the studio. Often they have been brought there from half way around the world: a tactic which flavours the transcendant moment of surprise when the 'guests' are recognised – and helps to disguise the cheapness of such programmes. It does little, however, to help the excruciating moment of silence which tends to fall *after* the long-lost friends have been re-introduced.

Surprise, Surprise! and *This Is Your Life* are not the only programmes built around the reunion. *TV-am* has a special slot, while a more sober version of reunion fever can also be seen in *Newsnight*, *Forty Minutes* and *First Tuesday*: recently, the device of reunion has heightened issues from the atomic bomb and Nazi Germany to juvenile delinquency. The dramatic moment of

101

intensity beloved by *Surprise, Surprise!* is replaced by a gentler, more measured summoning up of feeling and identification, but the emotional hook offered by the strategy remains unchanged.

At some point in all these programmes, the interviewers will ask how the re-unitees *feel* about what has happened to them. This is *the* enquiry put to real people: whether they have won a holiday on a game show or lost a husband in a bomb explosion, the same phrase will inevitably emerge. They are hardly ever asked what they *think* – a question normally reserved for bona fide experts. Television professionals know they need passion from real people, not a fluency with data or a grasp of abstract ideas. John Percival, who worked on *Man Alive* says, 'One of the great sadnesses to a documentary producer is that people will rehearse the facts, going over and over them in a very laborious way. That's not what the producer wants: he can tell you that in 25 seconds' worth of commentary'.

Ted Barham, a long-time campaigner for pensioners' rights, discovered these strictures for himself when he was interviewed by *Channel Four News* about the Fowler Review of Pensions. Speaking later on *Right To Reply*, he complained that his analysis of the Review had not been included – but the few, rather sad, comments he made about his own financial situation had been. This was embarrassing, he said, because it looked as though he was begging: and, indeed, someone sent him some money for a holiday. *Channel Four News* replied they 'wanted to give some idea of the circumstances of people who have to rely on the welfare state. The political issues raised by the Fowler Review were dealt with at some length elsewhere in the programme.' But Ted Barham was not arguing about the coverage the Review received: he minded his pre-ordained role as a depressed, miserable old man. Rather than being used passively to provide an emotional edge to an expert's thesis by describing how being a pensioner *feels*, he wanted a chance actively to use his knowledge.

Television became adept at capitalising on the audience-grabbing potential of real people's emotion in the 60's and 70's. Aided by new fast film stock and light-weight cameras which made location shooting more flexible, programmes like *This Week* and *Man Alive* homed in on 'difficult' areas of sexual and social life. Abortion, adultery, suicide, marital breakdown: all were fearlessly exposed to the camera. The then-standard tactic of having cool and distanced experts pick over such issues in a studio was eschewed by *Man Alive* – at least for the first phase of its existence. Instead, Desmond Wilcox and his production team concentrated on highly personal interviews with ordinary people, going for their viewers' jugulars with relentless and frequently gruelling displays of private pain. Crying became *Man Alive*'s hallmark, to the extent that some critics jokingly dubbed it 'sob-umentary'. 'It was,' John Percival says, 'almost mandatory for someone to burst into tears on the programme.'

These characteristics mean that as well as being praised as compulsive television, the *Man Alive* tradition has also been vigorously attacked. Emotional documentaries of this school exploit real people, some newspaper critics argue, by turning their most private moments of grief into a public spectacle. It is a dubious and potentially corrupt practice, they say, to take intense, personal feelings and broadcast them as an entertaining diversion. Television professionals have also lately been at pains to distance themselves from this approach: a *Guardian* interview with Debbie Christie about the series she produced on the miners' strike included her comments on the 'mawkish and obtrusive... *Man Alive* school. You know, wait-for-the-tears-telly. Could you cry one more time for the camera while you tell us how you used to beat the children?'

John Percival, reporter on several of *Man Alive*'s most heart-wrenching films, now has similar qualms. 'The bad thing about *Man Alive* was that there were times when it made entertainment out of people's anguish. It is justifiable to show anguish if we think

A Kind of Living: a typical Man Alive. **Stirring social commentary or sob-umentary?**

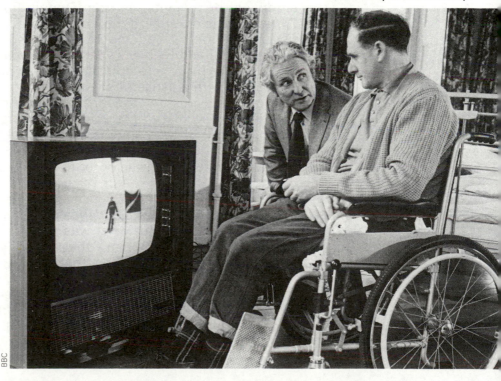

this person's pain needs to be communicated to the world. But, if we show it because we know it will make jolly good box, we should look at ourselves very carefully. In retrospect, I've wondered about my own motivation for making some of those films. Was I really so concerned about fulfilling social needs? Maybe I was more worried about making an entertaining, provocative, programme.'

Udi Eichler, producer of emotional documentaries for Thames during the 70's, also has misgivings. 'At the time, I found it a considerable triumph to have been able to provoke those raw emotions and then capture them on camera.' Now, he is not so confident. 'The turning point was when I was responsible for making a film about my home, a community where I had lived for many years. Being on the receiving end of television's attention was an intolerably painful experience. Most producers and directors have the gift to manipulate the situation psychologically: it is a capacity which can be terribly mis-used. People can do things which turn out to be terribly self-destructive. I still believe that there is a place for television of this kind, but I just can't do it any longer. I've solved the problem for myself by employing brash young people who are still full of energy and don't have the same personal difficulty in going out and manipulating people for their own ends.'

Udi Eichler's films triggered a particularly harsh attack on emotional documentaries from Dennis Potter, then *The Sunday Times*' television critic. Potter castigated what he dubbed as the 'Thames school of documentaries' for 'sociological sensational-ism' and claimed Eichler's *Marriage Guidance* was a 'vulgar and specious' intrusion into human misery. 'It ought,' he said, 'to leave its makers with a sense of shame at their own effrontery.' When, days later, the press release for a *This Week* documentary (about an emergency psychiatric intervention unit) promised a man breaking down in front of the cameras, Potter declined to watch. That, at least, he said, was an experience which people should be allowed to have without the intrusion of the camera.

David Cohen, the director of the programme in question, was unrepentant. He wrote in the television trade paper *Broadcast* that 'the merit of *Marriage Guidance* was how raw it was. It was shocking in places. But what was shocking was not the way the people felt about each other – that was truly pathetic, if anything – but rather the fact that they should be willing to explore their feelings so publicly. That this was shocking does not reflect on life in general, but on the limited sort of life we see on television. By a curious paradox, the box remains the only art form in which it is still possible to shock … If television is to remain an honest medium, it has to be willing to show things at their most painful.'

But is the desire for 'honesty' really the whole story about the

Long before Man Alive **and** The Marriage**, the thirties feature films** Television Spy **suggested that TV could be a voyeur.**

104

105

TELEVISION SPY

WITH
WILLIAM HENRY · JUDITH BARRETT
WILLIAM COLLIER, Sr.
· ANTHONY QUINN · RICHARD DENNING
Screen Play by Horace McCoy, William R. Lipman and Lillie Hayward
Directed by EDWARD DMYTRYK
A PARAMOUNT PICTURE

making (and watching) of programmes like **The Marriage**? **Spitting Image** introduced another perspective when it showed Desmond Wilcox snuggling up in bed with Marc and Karen in a spoof entitled **The Voyeur**. Are we all Peeping Toms, as the rubbery figures wickedly suggest?

Documentaries don't offer the titillation real voyeurs want from their secret looking: and, indeed, the interrupted, domestic nature of most television viewing doesn't encourage sexual reverie. The majority of programmes do, however, allow their viewers to believe they are watching something spontaneous. All the rigmarole of production – cameras, lights, crew – is disguised with an almost fetishistic ardour. This helps to reassure us that the people we are watching would have been sobbing or arguing or making fools of themselves even if the crew wasn't there. As we lap up the spectacle, we can admonish the lack of restraint of those providing it, safe in the belief that we would never behave in that way. And of course, horrible depravity is much more fun to spy on than respectable moderation.

These lascivious double-standards were much in evidence in the tabloids' reactions to **The Marriage**. The papers announced themselves appalled by the 'naive, stupid and simple' behaviour of 'show-offs' Marc and Karen: and then proceeded to make a hearty meal of the series' revelations. Especially convoluted doublethink could be seen in a **Daily Express** article with the headline 'Show-offs? Not Us, Say Bare-all Stars of **Marriage**'. The feature began with an attack on the couple's Fleet Street critics, thereby damning Marc, Karen **and** the writers' colleagues . . . and ended with a blob highlighting the fact that 'in tomorrow night's episode Marc displays his naked bottom as he is seen bathing.'

Desmond Wilcox responded by roundly lambasting what he called 'vulture's feast journalism'. This righteous indignation was a touch disingenuous. The BBC may not have told blatant untruths about the couple, as some of the tabloids did, but it had little hesitancy about showing a gloating nation what Desmond Wilcox called a 'refreshingly uninhibited young couple who . . . didn't mind talking freely about sex, their emotions, or love.' As **The Observer** put it, the BBC 'have no cause for smugness . . . They cook the joint, take the first slices and leave it on the sideboard; it can't be too much of a surprise that the rat-pack has a sense of smell.'

GETTING THE PERFORMANCE

A television programme is not something natural which 'just happens'. Neither does the camera simply record 'ordinary life', as the presence of the crew inevitably affects the people and events they are there to record. As Udi Eichler says, 'Being in a documentary means the invasion of your life, your home, your work situation, by a camera and a large team of people. That has got to become more important than the thing you are supposedly there to talk about. There is a huge paradox in encouraging people to 'be themselves' on camera: it is my job to persuade them to ignore this bizarre experience going on around them and behave as if I wasn't there.'

Directors of the *cinema verité* school attempt to get round these problems with unobtrusive equipment, a small crew and, not least, the financial resources which allow them to film over a long period. Even then Roger Graef, one of the foremost proponents of the approach, says, 'We don't claim to show events as they would have happened without us being there – merely that we kept our presence at all times to a minimum and therefore events resemble more closely what would have happened if the camera had been a fly on the wall.' *Cinema-verité* hardly dispenses with all the problems of film-making, though. Some people learn to ignore the presence of the crew, but by no means all do: Rosalind Brunt, a participant in Graef's *Decision*, on the Communist Party, said later that she was acutely aware of the need to perform as a 'good communist' for the film crew. Nor, as we shall see, do *verite* methods dispense with the issues raised by the editing process.

Other film-makers have suggested that there is a difference between trying to record what happens in front of the camera as honestly as possible and a more abstract commitment to showing some sort of 'general truth' about a situation. The problem with the latter course is trying to guarantee that 'general truths' will emerge on the days designated for the immensely expensive business of filming. As ex-*verité* director Angela Pope points out, 'however complete (a film-maker's) knowledge of his subject, however thorough his research, he is always the victim of happenstance. As

107

BBC-1

The film-maker as fly-on-the-wall? Roger Graef's Police series, one of several *verite* investigations into the hidden worlds inside organisation.

he flattens himself against the wall, chewing his nails, he can only hope that what he thinks **should** happen **will** happen. And if it does happen he can only hope his cameraman will be deft enough to capture it.'

Angela Pope's own, somewhat controversial, solution to these problems has been to give carefully staged reconstructions the look of *cinema verité*. This is an extreme version of the method the majority of directors find themselves forced to employ: rather than relying on careful planning and crossed fingers alone, most do a certain amount of what purists call 'cheating'. Scenes missed when film or sound ran out are re-enacted, obscured dialogue repeated, small moments – someone gardening, or making a cup of tea – staged to provide visuals to accompany voice-over explanation. And almost all programmes – *verité* included – depend on the device of the cutaway shot to join pieces of dialogue 'seamlessly' together. To avoid an awkward jump in the image the editor interposes another image, usually a 'noddy' shot of someone apparently responding to the speaker.

When it comes to the actual performances of the real people, however, some directors are unwilling to tutor their 'cast' too directly, being scared that over-theatrical performances will forfeit the precious 'texture of realness'. Some go as far as deliberately shunning contact with interviewees, hiding out of sight until the cameras are ready to roll.

Others follow Mike Russell Hills in going for 'a kind of conditioned response rather than an absolutely spontaneous one'. Without directly giving instructions they gently nudge and encourage their subjects along the road to 'realness', hoping that, in time, a correctly selected interviewee will produce what is required of him or her. For instance, Caroline Pick says 'I go in with particular areas in mind, narrowed down from what we discussed in the research interview. Then before we start I'll say, "Remember you spoke about this or that: it'd be really nice if you said that again." Although it looks fresh and in their own words, you are in fact artificially recreating the moment when you first met. On one hand that is manipulative, but I think I'm also enabling them to tell their story in a better way.'

Here too, financial constraints play their part in determining the procedure used, as John Percival points out. 'It all depends how many rolls of film you have to spare. If you have all the time in the world and a large budget, it probably pays to let an interviewee do it their way and eat up endless film. If time and money are pressing you have to chase people to keep them on the point. But you can't chase them too much, or they'll very quickly stop co-operating.'

The Price is Right's key to producing natural performances is its

elaborate physical environment. Bright lights, expensive, glittering backdrops, excited warm-up routines and loud music help to nurture a rowdy, uninhibited party atmosphere. Ideally, the participants then forget that they are in the studio. William G. Stewart says 'We leave them alone, let them enjoy it, let them join in, which is what they have come to do. Most TV audiences are rolling in the aisles at the warm-up man when some idiotic floor manager comes on and says "Quiet please everyone". The poor cast spend the next ten minutes bringing them back to life. *The Price is Right* is the only programme that doesn't inhibit people and make them behave like a "TV audience".'

None of this mood-enhancement is available to the vox pop directors who spend their time out in the street trying to encourage passers-by into the right quotation about a brand of catfood or a political party. The selection of interviewees must be made, trust established, the individual's understandable nervousness of the technology overcome and the appropriate lines delivered in an encounter lasting ten minutes at the most. The vox pop is film-making in microcosm.

Like William G. Stewart, and in a different way, Roger Graef, Mike Russell Hills finds that making the equipment as invisible as possible helps encourage the right kind of performance. 'I use a series of physical tricks to make the film crew a less frightening sight,' he says. 'Chiefly, I increase the physical distance between them and the camera with long lenses. All non-essential personnel are stuck as far away as possible: I sit the sound man on a wall. Sometimes I'll even put the mike down the back of my sleeve so that they are talking to my hand.'

Although he tries to make the technology of film-making appear friendly to his interviewees, a more combative side to the relationship between directors and real people hovers just beneath the surface. The camera, he says, is also 'a secret weapon'. 'If you walk up with the camera running it is easier for them to answer your question than fight you: the damage has been done.'

Immediately after the initial pick-up, Mike Russell Hills begins constructing a rapport between himself and the real person. 'I always start off by distancing myself from the crew. I say "Don't mind that bunch of yobbos over there, they just want to go down the pub." Then they start to feel like it's me and them against the rest.'

'Sometimes, to speed things up, I have two or three accomplices who work as my pimps and do a rounding up operation. It's their job to make friends with people. They walk up to a woman and say "Excuse me..." Then they'll switch to whatever she's like. Their voices will change: they can either act jokey, like it is all just a bit of fun, or play it very serious.

'When it comes to the actual chat I have a pretty clear idea of what I want from them. I blinker the conversation to keep it on a very narrow path, rather than letting them ramble on forever. Yes, you do help them phrase what they are trying to say. But you can't cheat. Regardless of the IBA rules, most real people wouldn't lie even if you waved money around in their face. And, anyway, if you encourage someone to say something they don't really believe, it shows in their face. So it wouldn't do you any good in any case.' Once again, the crucial issue is to get people to communicate realness.

According to Mike Russell Hills, part of the art of getting a good performance from real people is to magnify your interest in them. 'You have to be what used to be called a "cocktail party charmer". In fact, that just means being a good listener and reacting a lot. What you need is the ability to make people feel interesting, or intelligent, or beautiful, just by exaggerating your response to them.'

The same flattering and peculiarly intense, almost sexual, interest is also essential in the emotional documentary. David Cohen compares the relationship between film-maker and real person to a one night stand, saying it is a 'little bit like seduction and a little bit like therapy'.

All the same, too much emphasis on these licentious metaphors can detract attention from the feminine, almost motherly, solicitousness offered by most interviewers. It is no accident that the vast majority of researchers, who do the initial 'luring' of real people, are female.

John Percival says 'Anyone working in this kind of television must have the skill of listening. If you want people to talk about their feelings and their inner lives, things that are really important to them, you have to give them your total attention." On **Man Alive** a careful manipulation of this rapport aided the production of the requisite amount of tears: ideally, on the fifth and final roll of film. 'Very simply, one technique for getting people to cry on camera is to listen very sympathetically to what they have to say, asking questions which linger on the pain of their experience. A great deal of sympathy is expressed. Then, at some point, a silence is allowed to fall. You wait. Eventually, the person will weep as much to fill the void as anything else. Then you swiftly stop them weeping: even on **Man Alive** it was embarrassing if it went on too long. Today, getting people to actually cry is regarded as too obtrusive. What a producer has to do now is to get the person to the brink of bursting into tears without letting them do so. It is more effective.'

The heightened relationship helps the real person to forget about the presence of the camera. With assiduous attention from

the questioner, the interviewee will appear to be telling their story to a single individual, rather than to the eight or so people in the crew and the millions of viewers. For the viewer at home, the effect is of a pleasurably moving one-to-one intimacy.

However, this intimacy can become a problem if people start performing. Mike Russell Hills says 'You have to stop them from trying too hard to please you. If you're not careful they'll start chucking ad-speak around. They'll say "Oh, it's delicious because it has those big meaty chunks" – the sort of stuff people never say. They think that's what you want.' The father of the family in crisis who featured in Roger Graef's documentary *The Space Between Words* wrote that 'When filming started I thought our uneventful life was not producing any usable material. If the crew failed to turn up for a few days we wondered if we should offer to try harder – whatever that might mean.'

On occasion, the intensity of the relationship can have explosive consequences for the film-maker's subjects. Feelings of obligation to 'their friend', the director, may result in them being persuaded, against their better judgement, into making damaging personal revelations. Alternatively, the director may become too important in their lives. As John Percival says, 'being on television can be a very important experience, especially if you are talking about something emotional. For the person concerned it is a once in a life-time experience, but the producer goes on to do another job the next day. It becomes a great responsibility, especially if filming goes on over a period of weeks or months. The relationship can become a central part of the person's life and they can suffer an acute sense of deprivation and loss when it goes away.' When the marriage at the centre of *The Marriage* looked like running into trouble after Marc's encounter with an old girlfriend, he tele-phoned Desmond Wilcox in the middle of the night. How will Marc and Karen cope with married life when they no longer have the BBC as guide?

Most people appear in documentaries because they think it will be of assistance: either to themselves, or to some viewer they do not know. David Cohen has written that 'It is not hard to convince would-be contributors that to reveal their pain or distress on the box can, in fact, help others. Many people believe in causes like a more open attitude to homosexuality or to mental illness. They are willing to expose themselves to appearing because they feel – and any decent researcher will encourage them to feel – that what they are about to reveal may be useful in changing attitudes.'

In many cases this is true. But there are also instances where the proposal can border on the dishonest. John Percival says 'If you make social concern programmes you go around saying to people,

"I want you to appear and talk about something which is essentially private, because by doing so you may help other people." This can be a specious argument: the main purpose of TV is to entertain, not to help anybody.' David Cohen goes on to suggest that 'if television is to remain an honest medium, it has to be willing to show things at their most painful, without the get out of saying that the programme is directly helpful and suggests how you can cope with the pain.'

If real people are persuaded to appear on the grounds that television will help them with their problems, they can become badly disillusioned when they realise that television is not a cure-all panacea. When researcher Penny Webb interviewed people who had talked about their personal problems on television she found that a majority had expected more specific counselling than they received. Several felt they should have been warned against using television to get revenge on an erring partner. Public exposure can aggravate a crisis rather than healing it, as some found out to their cost.

Others found talking personally, or even crying, on television a productive and cathartic experience. Regardless of the director's ultimate intentions, their interest provides many people with an all-too-rare occasion to speak at length about their lives. Being listened to makes people feel their lives are important: that they matter. As Udi Eichler says, 'one of the incidental side-effects of television is that it can fulfil a desperate need for attention which is lacking in some people's lives.'

Several people who replied to an advertisement in **Competitors Journal** which asked for accounts of their experiences on gameshows seemed to have similar motives. One rather poignant letter begins 'Although I am a qualified physiotherapist at the moment I am a housewife with two small boys (aged three and 11) to look after. So though I am always busy, life can get routine.' She says the show made her feel 'almost like royalty' and that 'As the train pulled out of Newcastle, back across the Tyne, I was really looking forward to seeing my family, but there was a real lump in my throat. But I shall always have the memory of that very special day.'

Difficult as it may be to remember, contestants are also viewers. A week after they appear, they will watch an almost identical programme, with other people taking the contestants' roles. As we saw in Chapter Two, television is an important social ritual and emotional point of reference for many of its viewers. Being on television, even if in only a very constrained and peripheral role, allows the viewer to pursue this relationship a stage further. After all, the celebratory photograph of contestants with Leslie Crowther given to winners of **The Price is Right** is almost tailor-made to be placed on top of a television set.

Going to the studio, chatting momentarily with stars, seeing the make-up areas and canteen, having drinks in the hospitality rooms: these were the experiences most avidly reported in the *Competitor's Journal* letters. A few commented on the pleasure of feeling that they, for a brief while, were **necessary** to television. Usually it is television that gives the presents and acts as provider. Swapping sides of the screen meant that, for once, the viewer is able to offer assistance, to 'help television out', as one contestant put it. Real people may want prizes, attention and fame, but somewhere at the centre of their motivation also lies the fact that they like watching television and, particularly, the way watching television makes them feel. Accordingly, they appreciate the opportunity, however brief, to be part of TV.

TELLING STORIES

In an article in *The Radio Times* before the first instalment of *The Marriage* Desmond Wilcox said that the film contained scenes 'reminiscent of *Dallas*'. Making it, he said, had proved to him that 'real life *is* soap opera'. Later, he retreated: when the tabloids were

113

The marriage in The Marriage: probably 1986's most notorious and most watched documentary series. But just what was its attraction?

BBC Desmond Wilcox

after his blood, he complained that Marc and Karen **weren't EastEnders** or **Coronation Street** actors, so why all the interest?

However much Desmond Wilcox may have regretted those early statements, the fact is that **The Marriage** and the majority of other documentaries **are** designed to give viewers many of the same pleasures they get from fiction. Excitement, empathy, emotion (which, as we have seen, real people are well qualified to give) a feeling of realness, a look inside someone else's life, and 'a good, human story' – **Brookside**, **Emmerdale Farm**, **Man Alive** and **Forty Minutes** all offer these.

A documentary which simply showed pieces of real life would be unlikely to have this gripping quality. It is the organisation of the ingredients which counts: how they are assembled into a narrative which reveals a story. The tale may be the unfolding of an event, like **The Marriage**, or the solving of a problem. Frequently, these stories work by posing an enigma and then making us wait to find out the answer. **Dallas** wanted us to ask 'Who shot JR?'. A campaigning documentary, meanwhile, will want us to wonder **if** a homeless family will get the flat they need. It is the possibility of finding some kind of resolution to the question which grabs our interest and feelings: not simply the chance to find out facts.

Udi Eichler says, 'Whether you are talking about drama, or sport or documentary, television has remarkably similar narrative rules. "Good television" is telling a good story. You make something good by using whatever raw material you have to tell a story that will hold its audience through a beginning, a middle and an end. And, because of that, the documentary maker is never giving you real life because that would be sprawly, boring, slovenly and full of irrelevancies. When the documentary maker shapes his raw material he does it with just as much skill as a brilliant script writer or a great feature film director.'

Film-makers have sometimes compared themselves to sculptors hacking away at the excess material to create the form they are looking for. Cartloads of excess have to be discarded before they find the right shape. The metaphor is a touch pretentious, but also in some ways accurate: non-fiction directors do continually have to whittle away at the messy, over-abundant surface of life. Decisions have to be taken about what tiny segments of life will be snatched by the camera: then, in the cutting room, they and the editor must further reduce down hours of 'rushes' in order to produce the particular narrative they have chosen to focus on.

This process of constructing a narrative lies at the heart of documentary film-making: even in **verité** films, which the makers like to believe closely approximate 'real life'. In a conversation with some of his collaborators, Terence Twigg, the editor of many of

114

Roger Graef's films, suggests 'you have to discover for yourself what the story is. The people (you are filming) are not always certain what the story is. In a sense this is where your rules fall apart, because you are proceeding, in fact, to structure your material.' When individuals agree to perform as real people, they are accepting that the fabric of their existence is going to be re-jigged by somebody else. The parts of their life which the film-maker decides are humdrum or repetitious are cut out, or reshaped and polished to highlight the elements that have been categorised as important. Watching at home, we will never know what was discarded on the cutting room floor. As John Percival said while being interviewed on camera, 'The big issue is editing: what do you do with all the material you have captured on film? The potentially damaging thing about this situation is that when you edit what I'm saying, you'll do it the way you want it.'

The film-maker decides what the story is – not the real person. Sometimes, as with Roger Graef's team, the narrative will be derived from the circumstances of the individual life. More often, the narrative will be already formed in the director's mind: the interviewee is required to provide an illustration of a pre-existing thesis. As Caroline Pick says, real people are useful to the film-maker only when 'their story slots into your jigsaw'. All the other potential narratives in a person's life will be temporarily put to one side, a red herring in the path of the question the director has decided to follow. You may end up feeling, in Laurie Taylors' words, 'just a comma in some editor's cutting room ... someone with no history, no context, just thirty feet of film bunged in the middle of nowhere.' Individuals whose stories go against the grain of the overall narrative will be written out, or consigned to the tray marked 'awkward examples', just as Desmond Wilcox did with couples who had been married before, not been married long enough, had too much money or in some other way seemed a-typical to him.

On occasion, this can lead to the over-representation of an atypical stereotype. There are rumours of researchers from London spending hours looking for a 'real Northerner' with a flat cap, roll-up and an evocative, but almost impossible to find, **Coronation Street**-type house. Articulate, conservative, blacks are not much in demand for programmes on the inner-cities; young Rastafarians are, since some television journalists believe they 'stand in' more readily as typical representatives of their race.

The most serious complaints occur in cases where people feel that the film-maker's narrative radically contradicts their own view of a situation. This was the case with the striking miners who disagreed with the type of questions television was asking about the strike. Their narratives centred on the future of the coal-mining

communities and the struggle to survive the hardships of the strike. Television, by and large, was especially interested in picket-line violence and the so-called drift back to work. In particular, these narratives tended to concern individual, personal stories: a single family's struggle, the traumas of a solitary working miner, the future of Arthur Scargill. More abstract, political issues, such as the long-term reasons behind Mrs Thatcher's attack on the coal industry were not given the same attention. These narratives lacked the obviously engaging quality and visual simplicity of a personal story, and offered fewer opportunities for the intimate and emotional styles of television normally associated with real people. As a result, these crucial issues were, on the whole, simply ignored.

For the miners, these problems were aggravated by television's history of interpreting working-class lives for the benefit of its middle-class viewers. Sometimes, especially in the 50's, the effort put into explanation almost amounted to translation from a foreign language. This was literally the case on those occasions where a presenter with correct BBC pronunciation was brought in to read a working-class subject's words in voice-over.

Often the justifications for such practices were soundly liberal: the working classes were put under the microscope in order to expose inequalities, campaign for better housing, or jobs, or welfare benefits. It was, and still is, important to increase the simple, numerical representations of working people on television, and clearly it is valuable to illuminate the diversity of how people live. All the same, these obviously laudable motives often come tinged with the unhealthy fascination with squalor and depravity which stained Victorian philanthropy and Orwell's **The Road to Wigan Pier** alike.

This heady combination of 'good works' and disdain was taken up by the programmes in the **Man Alive** tradition. And, just like their distinguished forebears, their favourite stories concern pitiful victims. Good-hearted little match girls and diminutive chimney sweeps have been replaced by other groups of people crushed by life. But there is never only one potential narrative to be used to illuminate a situation: there are always other, alternative, stories that could be told. As Caroline Pick says, 'I can't bear films that just make people look like victims. When I'm selecting interviewees, I try to find people who believe it is possible to change things. Otherwise, everything just looks hopeless: endless terrible things happening, people suffering, and no way to change it. Obviously it is worth exposing these problems, but you have also to get across the idea that things could possibly change.'

Some film-makers attempt to circumvent these issues by working more closely with the people they are filming. Work-in-progress is shown to the people involved, and their comments incorporated into the film-making process. But it is unlikely that these refinements can ever alter the fundamental power relationship between film-maker and real person. The evidence from film-makers is that, on the whole, people don't object, even when they might be expected to. If the 'seduction' by the film-maker has been thorough, the real people may well defer to the director's judgement about what should be shown. When complaints are made, they are usually to do with the personal objectives the real person brought to the film-making, rather than the underlying ethos of the programme. An emotional attack on a spouse may be regretted, but the deeper questions raised by a particular narrative

Displaying the awards. Are these really the main motivation for contestants?

which presented all divorcees as suffering victims will probably not be disputed.

This does not mean, however, that real people are completely powerless. Television wants something from them: because of that they can, occasionally manipulate that need to their own ends. Some real people try to use light entertainment programmes to promote themselves as mini-stars. A few succeed: Annie Mizzen, the enthusiastic old lady who became a fixture on *That's Life* vox pop's was one. A tiny number cross the line entirely and become professionals: Fred Dibnah, the steeplejack and Fred Housego, the taxi-driver winner of *Mastermind*, are the most well-known.

Real people can also use their appearance to win political points. The Glasgow Media Group has frequently pointed out that strikers interviewed for news bulletins outside factory gates are at a disadvantage compared to their bosses, who will tend to be interviewed in a plush office. Certainly the striker's presence will not be endowed with any of the classic symbols of television authority, such as rows of distinguished looking books. They may have to think on their feet while their boss might get a calmer, more leisurely interview: if the striker is interviewed outside, the sound quality undoubtedly will be worse. But none of this is necessarily a tragedy. In some cases, and to some viewers, these elements will make the striker 'speak' as more honest and direct than their boss.

Even if the surrounding commentary labels them as extraordinary – an extremist, or troublemaker – their presentation will signal them as representatives of ordinariness. That they will probably be working class and might have a regional accent and working clothes, will predispose some viewers, at least, to listen favourably to them.

Although television makes much of the democracy of having members of the public put their questions to official figures, real people are often little more than stooges for the politicians. Members of the audience of **Question Time** rarely manage more than a general and obvious point before being despatched by

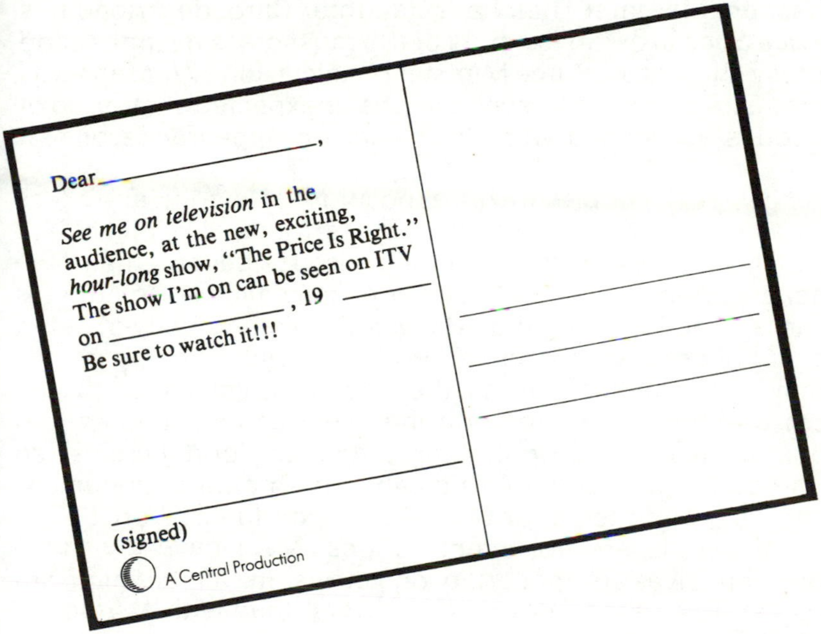

The card The Price is Right contestants can send to their friends.

Dear_____,

See me on television in the audience, at the new, exciting, *hour-long* show, "The Price Is Right." The show I'm on can be seen on ITV on _____, 19 _____
Be sure to watch it!!!

(signed)

A Central Production

Robin Day. All the same, these occasions do involve a certain amount of risk for the television institution. Despite careful pre-selection, there is no way producers can guarantee real people won't puncture the unwritten codes of deference and protocol which lie at the heart of political broadcasting. And when Diana Gould appeared on a **Nationwide Election Special**, she did exactly that.

Mrs Gould, a Gloucestershire teacher, used the programme to cross-examine Margaret Thatcher on the sinking of the Argentinian cruiser **General Belgrano** during the Falklands war. With the aid of a precise, unflappable manner, and an encyclopaedic knowledge of the facts, she managed to throw the Prime Minister into considerable confusion.

To many watching, the excitement of the confrontation was emphasised by the fact that Mrs Gould was pre-eminently a real person. Her grey hair, sensible clothes and kindly, but no-nonsense, schoolmistress' manner all backed up her case: here, many people felt, really was a representative of ordinary good sense. To many of the Prime Minister's supporters this was manifestly unfair: real people are not supposed to deal with facts at all, never mind be confident and articulate with them. The question of whether Mrs Gould was a genuine 'real person' became a political hot potato: according to Tory MP Tom King, Diana Gould was *Belgrano* campaigner Tam Dalyell 'in drag'. In her book, *Diary of an Election*, Margaret Thatcher's daughter Carol described this *Nationwide Special* as 'an example of the most crass nastiness and discourtesy shown to a Prime Minister on television'. What she was really protesting about, however, was the unexpected shattering of all the codes associated with the television appearance of real people.

Ultimately, real people are in a position of significantly less power than the presenters. Except in very rare cases like that of Mrs Gould, their opinions are not sought on issues beyond their own personal experience. Neither are they usually allowed to address the camera directly, as she did. Many suffer the indignity of being slotted, out of context, into someone else's thesis; of being gently, but firmly, manhandled around the floor of gameshows by the compère and hostesses. Vox pop interviewees are pumped and guided into saying the right things, and as John Percival so forcefully points out, some participants in emotional documentaries are pushed to tears for the sake of 'good television'.

But, real people are not simply dupes. Most have their own personal objectives in appearing on television: aims which are often more to do with their role as viewers, than with any desire for temporary stardom. They enter into an unspoken and one-sided bargain with television, agreeing to 'play the game' by 'acting naturally', letting their emotions show and ignoring the camera.

To television professionals, real people's feelings about the experience of appearing are of little importance. They are there to do a job: to provide an emotional validation for the arguments of experts, and spectacles of passion, happiness and pain. Once they have performed their role, they cease to matter. After editing, the footage will pass into the hands of the institution that commissioned it. Decisions will be taken about scheduling and promotion: areas in which the people filmed will not be considered. The film-makers themselves will start to worry about whether the production is regarded as a success in whatever sector of the television industry they happen to inhabit. They will be looking, in varying degrees, for critical esteem, good appreciation index ratings and high viewing figures. Soon afterwards, they will move on to the next production. The sales departments of their companies' head offices will take over, looking for overseas revenue or, in the case of game shows, the possibility of a 'format deal' for other countries to produce their own version of the show. The subjects of this industry, meanwhile, will settle down as viewers to watch themselves in their own sitting rooms, their old relationship, if not their old attitudes, to the medium re-established.

The moment when 'real person' Diana Gould challenged Margaret Thatcher on a Nationwide Special was important enough to be commemorated in a special booklet.

BIBLIOGRAPHY

CHAPTER ONE

Belson, William A. *Television Violence and the Adolescent Boy*, Saxon House, Farnborough, 1978

Ferguson, Bob. "Children's Television: The Germination of Ideology" in Lusted, David and Drummond, Philip (ed) *TV and Schooling* British Film Institute, London, 1985.

Ferguson, Bob. "Black Blue Peter" in Len Masterman, (ed) *Television Mythologies*, Comedia, London, 1985.

Murdock, Graham and McCron, Robin. "The Television and Delinquency Debate", *Screen Education*, No 30, Spring 1979.

Smith, Joan. "Mrs Whitehouse's Private Member", *New Statesman*, 13th December, 1985.

Winn, Marie. *The Plug In Drug*, Penguin, Harmondsworth, 1977.

Winn, Marie. *Children Without Childhood*, Penguin, Harmondsworth, 1981.

CHAPTER TWO

Brunsdon, Charlotte. "Writing About Television Soap Opera" in Len Masterman, (ed) *Television Mythologies*, Comedia, London, 1985.

Collett, Peter and Lamb, Roger. *Watching People Watching Television* unpublished report to the IBA. 1985.

Dyer, Richard. *Stars*, British Film Institute, London, 1979.

Dyer, Richard. "Taking Popular Television Seriously" in Lusted, David and Drummond, Philip (ed) *TV and Schooling*, British Film Institute, London, 1985.

Eaton, Mick. "Television Situation Comedy" in Bennett, Tony, et al (eds) *Popular Television and Film*, British Film Institute, London, 1981.

Ellis, John. *Visible Fictions*, Routledge and Kegan Paul, London, 1982.

Eng, Ien. *Watching Dallas*, Methuen, London 1982.

Geraghty, Christine. "The Continuous Serial—A Definition" in Dyer, Richard et al (eds) *Coronation Street*, British Film Institute, London, 1981.

Goodhardt, G.J., Ehrenberg, A.S.C., and Collins, M.A. *The Television Audience: Patterns of Viewing*, Gower, Aldershot, 1975.

Hobson, Dorothy. *Crossroads—The Drama of a Soap Opera*, Methuen, London, 1982.

Lewis, Justin. "Decoding Television News" in Richard Collins et al (ed) *Television in Transition*, British Film Institute, London, 1986.

Morley, David. *The Nationwide Audience*, British Film Institute, London 1980.

Mills, Adam and Rice, Phil. "Quizzing the Popular", *Screen Education* no 41, Winter/Spring 1982.

Culture and Society

Paterson, Richard. "Planning The Family: The Art of the Television Schedule", *Screen Education* no 35, Summer 1980.

Pilsworth, Michael. " 'An Imperfect Art'—TV Scheduling in Britain", *Sight and Sound*.

Taylor, Laurie and Mullan, Bob. *Univited Guests*, Chatto and Windus,

London, 1986.
Williams, Raymond. *Television, Technology and Cultural Form*, Fontana/Collins, London, 1974.

C H A P T E R   T H R E E

Black, Peter. *The Mirror in the Corner*, Hutchinson, London, 1982.
Dyer, Richard. *Light Entertainment*, British Film Institute, London, 1973.
Dyer, Richard. "Entertainment and Utopia", Movie no 24
Hoggart, Richard. *The Uses of Literacy*, Chatto and Windus, London, 1957.
Poole, Mike. "The Cult of the Generalist—British Television Criticism 1936-83", *Screen* vol 25 no 2, March-April 1984.
Hebdige, Dick. "Towards A Cartography of Taste", *Block* no 4, 1981.
Kerr, Paul. "Classic Serials—To Be Continued" *Screen* vol 23, no 1, May-June 1982.
Lealand, Geoffrey. *American Programmes on British Screens*, Broadcast Research Unit Working Paper, London, 1984.
Norman, Bruce. *Here's Looking at You*, BBC, London, 1984.
Poole, Michael. "The Case For the Defense", *Edinburgh International Television Festival Magazine, 1984.*

C H A P T E R   F O U R

Brunsdon, Charlotte and Morley, David. *Everyday Television: Nationwide*, British Film Institute, London, 1978.

Dimbleby, Jonathan. *Richard Dimbleby*, Hodder and Stoughton, London, 1975.
Goldie, Grace Wyndham. *Facing the Nation:Television and Politics 1936-79*, The Bodley Head, London, 1977.
Kumar, Krishan. "Holding the Middle Ground: the BBC, the public and the professional broadcaster", Curran, James, et al (eds) *Mass Communication and Society*, Edward Arnold, London, 1977.
Langer, John. "Television's Personality System", *Media, Culture and Society* vol 3 no 4, October 1981.
Petley, Julian. "Gurus: the cult of the TV personality", *Primetime* no 5, Spring 1983.
Marshall, Stuart. "The Image of Authority". *Framework*

C H A P T E R   F I V E

Cohen, David. "Should we let TV intrude on private emotion?", *Broadcast*, 29th August, 1977.
Glasgow University Media Group, *Bad News*, Routledge and Kegan Paul, London, 1976.
Gould, Diana. *On the Spot*. Cecil Woolf, London, 1984.
Pope, Angela. "A Representation of Reality", *The Listener*, 12th January 1984.
Swallow, Norman, *Factual Television*, Focal Press, London, 1966.
Wyver, John. *Nothing But the Truth: Cinema Verite and the Films of the Roger Graef Team*, ICA, London, 1982.
Vaughan, Dai. *Television Documentary Usage*, British Film Institute, 1976.

Videotapes of all six OPEN THE BOX programmes will be available from the British Film Institute Film & Video Library, 81 Dean Street, London W1V 6AA (01-437 4355) and from Guila Learning, Guild House, Peterborough PE2 9PZ (0733-315315). If you want to think further about the ideas in the programmes and discuss them in groups or on courses, the free booklet on OPEN THE BOX will be helpful. Containing notes on each of the six programmes and information for further reading, the booklet is available from Channel 4 and will also accompany the videos. For copies of this booklet please send a large SAE to Open The Box, PO Box 4000 at London W3 6XJ, or Glasgow G12 9JQ, or Belfast BT2 7FE.

Book List

Other titles from Comedia

No. 33 WOMEN, MEDIA, CRISIS: Femininity and Disorder by Michèle Mattelart
£4.95 paperback only

No. 32 PHOTOGRAPHIC PRACTICES: Towards a Different Image
edited by Stevie Bezencenet
£3.95 paperback, £10.50 hardback

No. 31 UNDERSTAINS: The Sense and Seduction of Advertising
by Kathy Myers
£5.95 paperback, £12.00 hardback

No. 30 BOYS FROM THE BLACKSTUFF: The Making of TV Drama
by Bob Millington and Robin Nelson
£5.95 paperback, £12.00 hardback

No. 29 THE STRUGGLE FOR BLACK ARTS IN BRITAIN by Kwesi Owusu
£4.95 paperback only

No. 28 FOURTH RATE ESTATE—An anatomy of Fleet Street by Tom Baistow
£3.95 paperback, £10.95 hardback

No. 27 THE YEARS OF THE WEEK by Patricia Cockburn
£6.95 paperback only

No. 26 TEACHING THE MEDIA by Len Masterman
£5.95 paperback, £12.00 hardback

No. 25 MAKING SENSE OF THE MEDIA—A 10-part media studies course by
Holly Goulden, John Hartley and Tim O'Sullivan
£25 paperback only

No. 24 TELEVISION MYTHOLOGIES—Stars, Shows and Signs
edited by Len Masterman
£3.95 paperback, £10.50 hardback

No. 23 COMMUNITY, ART AND THE STATE—a different prescription
by Owen Kelly
£3.95 paperback, £10.50 hardback

No. 9 NUKESPEAK—The media and the bomb edited by Crispin Aubrey
£2.50 paperback, £7.50 hardback

No. 8 NOT THE BBC/IBA—The case for community radio by Simon Partridge
£1.95 paperback, £5.00 hardback

No. 7 CHANGING THE WORLD—The printing industry in transition
by Alan Marshall
£3.50 paperback, £9.50 hardback

No. 6 THE REPUBLIC OF LETTERS—WORKING-class writing and local
publishing edited by David Morley and Ken Worpole
£3.95 paperback, £8.50 hardback

No. 5 NEWS LTD—Why you can't read all about it by Brain Whitaker
£3.95 paperback, £9.50 hardback

No. 4 ROLLING OUR OWN—Women as printers, publishers and distributors
by Eileen Cadman, Gail Chester, Agnes Pivot
£2.25 paperback only

No. 3 THE OTHER SECRET SERVICE—Press distribution and press
censorship by Liz Cooper, Charles Landry and Dave Berry
£1.20 paperback only

No. 2 WHERE IS THE OTHER NEWS—The news trade and the radical press
by Dave Berry, Liz Cooper and Charles Landry
£2.75 paperback only

No. 1 HERE IS THE OTHER NEWS—Challenges to the local commercial press
by Crispin Aubrey, Charles Landry and David Morley
£2.75 paperback only

126

Organizations and Democracy Series

No. 1 WHAT A WAY TO RUN A RAILROAD—an analysis of radical failure by
Charles Landry, David Morley, Russell Southwood and Patrick Wright
£2.50 paperback only

No. 2 ORGANIZING AROUND ENTHUSIASMS: Patterns of Mutual Aid in
Leisure by Jeff Bishop and Paul Hoggett
£5.95 paperback only

No. 3 BAD SOLUTIONS TO GOOD PROBLEMS: The Practice of
Organizational Change by Liam Walsh
£3.95 paperback only, Spring 1986